HAVE I TOLD YOU
THIS ALREADY?

ALSO BY LAUREN GRAHAM

Someday, Someday, Maybe

Talking as Fast as I Can

In Conclusion, Don't Worry About It

HAVE I TOLD YOU THIS ALREADY?

STORIES I DON'T WANT TO FORGET
TO REMEMBER

LAUREN GRAHAM

BALLANTINE BOOKS

New York

Published in the United States by Ballantine Books, an imprint of
Random House, a division of Penguin Random House LLC, New York.

BALLANTINE is a registered trademark and the colophon is a trademark
of Penguin Random House LLC.

Library of Congress Cataloging-in-Publication Data
Names: Graham, Lauren, author.
Title: Have I told you this already?: stories I don't want to forget to remember /
Lauren Graham.
Description: First edition. | New York: Ballantine Books, [2022] |
Identifiers: LCCN 2022022236 (print) | LCCN 2022022237 (ebook) |
ISBN 9780593355428 (hardcover) | ISBN 9780593355435 (ebook)
Subjects: LCSH: Graham, Lauren, 1967- |
Actors—United States—Biography. | LCGFT: Autobiographies.
Classification: LCC PN2287.G663 A3 2022 (print) |
LCC PN2287.G663 (ebook) |
DDC 791.4502/8092 [B]—dc23/eng/20220608
LC record available at https://lccn.loc.gov/2022022236
LC ebook record available at https://lccn.loc.gov/2022022237

Printed in the United States of America on acid-free paper

randomhousebooks.com

2 4 6 8 9 7 5 3

Book design by Alexis Capitini

For Graham (5), Tripp (3), Kit (2), Tucker (1),
and all the stories yet to be told

Contents

Introduction   xi

1. Ne Oublie   3

2. Boobs of the '90s   15

3. Ryan Gosling Cannot Confirm   31

4. R.I.P. Barneys New York   45

5. But I've Played One on TV   61

6. Old Lady Jackson Takes You to Dinner at 5 P.M.   77

7. Actor-y Factory   83

8. Health Camps I Have Hated (Yet in Most
   Cases Returned To)   99

CONTENTS

9. Forever 32   113

10. Squirrel Signs   123

11. Red Hat, Blue Hat   135

12. I Feel Bad About Nora Ephron's Neck   143

13. Marmalade   155

14. Mochi   163

15. New York Is a Person   175

Acknowledgments   185

Introduction

STORIES HAVE ALWAYS been important to me. As a kid, I lived for the stories my dad would tell me about his childhood growing up in Valley Stream, New York, where he'd hitchhike home from football practice in his Catholic school uniform. During my first few years of elementary school, I fell in love with reading and would read anything I could get my hands on as long as it was about a horse, or a girl who had a horse, or a girl who wanted a horse and got one even if she lived with her family in a small walk-up apartment in Manhattan. Eventually my interests expanded a bit, and in high school and college and in my graduate acting program I was thrilled to read everything from Jane Austen to the classics of dramatic literature to breezy novels intended to be read on a beach. When I graduated and first started working professionally here and there, I was excited to act in other people's stories, whether in a laundry detergent commercial or a small guest part on a show. Whether I was a mom who was worried about packing a nutritional lunch (one line in a Jiffy peanut butter commercial), or a student who was being asked about the homework assignment (three lines in the daytime drama *Loving*), I was living my dream of being a storyteller.

Eventually, I got some bigger parts with more complex tales to tell, and now that I'm in my 30s, I'm looking forward to all the stories that are yet to be—WAIT. WHAT? The legal department has just informed me that I'm not in my 30s anymore. How is that even possible? It seems like just yesterday that I was lying to all the casting people about being 28 because IMDb hadn't been invented yet and Google wasn't really a thing. It seems like just yesterday that I filmed all day in Los Angeles and then took a red-eye to New York in order to do a photo shoot after which I went to a U2 concert and went out after and flew back the next day and didn't feel tired at all. It seems like just yesterday that, on the very day I turned 32, I was cast as Lorelai in *Gilmore Girls,* a part that would change my life for the better. Oh, well. At least we have a brand-new season of *Gilmore Girls* to look forward to, and that way we can relive all the wondrous olden times togeth—WAIT. WHAT? Lawyers have just informed me that there is no new season of *Gilmore Girls* on the horizon, and I can be sued/canceled on Twitter for suggesting there is.

How is that even possible? What is this book even about if I'm not going to explain the final four words or tell you who's the father of Rory's baby?

If you've missed *Gilmore Girls,* the truth is that I've missed you too, and this book is one way of keeping our conversation going. I loved writing my last book of essays, *Talking as Fast as I Can,* and even without any new stories about the show, I found I had more to say. And if you've never seen *Gilmore Girls,* then you're in luck, because I'm mainly telling other stories here: about stuffing my bra for work, shoplifting by accident, what it's like being in a long-term relationship with New York City. (Spoiler: I love it, but it's expensive and doesn't always smell great.)

"Have I told you this already?" is a phrase I use so often that it's become a joke among my oldest and dearest friends and family. These are the people who've been there with me through bad breakups and failed exams and questionable haircuts and dinner parties that went into the wee hours, and I've been there through those things with them too. We've heard each other's stories over and over by now, but somehow we still can't wait to hear them again. These are friends who are such an essential part of my life that sometimes it's hard to remember if I've told them something already or if I've told them but they haven't heard the most recent version, or if they were actually with me when the whatever-it-was happened. These relationships are invaluable, and as I've gotten older I only value them more.

And you're part of this group too: you are people with

whom I've shared stories for so long now that in some cases I had to go back to my first book to make sure I hadn't told you some of them already. I'd like to take this opportunity to tell you how grateful I am to have you as a viewer and a reader and a GIF-maker and a whatever the thing is called where you film yourself lip-syncing entire scenes of mine on Instagram.

You're all the best!

HAVE I TOLD YOU
THIS ALREADY?

Ne Oublie

I'm certain I graduated from college, but I haven't seen my diploma in over twenty years. I can't find the parking ticket I got yesterday. It's probably sitting in the same drawer alongside the one I can't find from last week. At age 14, I remember holding my social security card for approximately five minutes before I misplaced it and never saw it again. Last week, I found a watch I thought I'd lost months ago inside of a shoe. Perhaps that's why I'm pretty good at memorizing lines of dialogue and people's phone numbers—I can't be counted on to save the paper I wrote them on, and even if I put the info into my phone, it might take me a while to remember where I left it. I lose my phone, my wallet, and my keys multiple times a day. Sometimes, I'll go into the kitchen to find that book I've been reading and two hours later I have organized the silverware drawer but have zero recollection of what I came into the kitchen for. "One fish goes this way, the other fish goes that way," is how a friend once described these absentminded tendencies. I am a Pisces, after all.

Possibly, I got it from my dad. Growing up, I didn't own a set of house keys. He probably lost his own set too many times before he gave up and decided it was easier just to leave the front door open (please don't break into my dad's house). As a teen, I was taught to leave car keys in the ignition, because how else was anyone supposed to find them? (Please don't steal my dad's car.) To this day, my father is well known for driving away with a coffee mug still on the roof of his car, and even though everyone in the family has bought him countless pairs of nicer sunglasses, the only ones he seems unable to lose are the neon-green mirrored ones intended for road biking.

But what my dad has lost in sets of keys, he's made up for with his ability to paint vivid pictures of the past. As a keeper of the objects and details of the present, his record may be spotty, but as a minder of memories, he excels.

My father is an excellent storyteller with a tight repertoire. If his stories were songs, he wouldn't have a ton of deep cuts, but he could fill an entire album of Greatest Hits. As a kid, I lived for the rotation of stories from his own childhood: the time he got separated from his mom in the grocery store and a neighbor found him and brought him home; the day his family became the first on the block to own a television; racing on the beaches of Long Island with his collie, King. Then there was an entire spinoff series about Dad and his childhood friend Georgie. Dad and Georgie taking the train to Coney Island to ride the Ferris wheel; Dad and Georgie dressing in trench coats and fedoras for their secret club in which they pretended to be Al Capone's henchmen; Dad and Georgie going to the soda shop, where they'd sit at the counter after football practice and order an egg cream or a "suicide" (an ice cream sundae involving a scoop of every available flavor).

As I got older, the stories matured as well. There was the one about his senior prom date, Angela, who'd fallen asleep under the sunlamp that day and came to the door beet red and puffy from crying, my father reassuring her he couldn't tell at all (he could tell). And the day he met my mom as she was moving into his same apartment building, and she asked if he wouldn't mind letting her make a call because her phone hadn't been hooked up yet. The year he spent after college in Vietnam working for the Agency for International Development, where the local kids would sometimes crawl under a cafe table where he was having lunch and pull at his leg hair, fascinated because they'd never seen such a thing.

One of my favorites, one I'd heard over and over since I was little, was about the day I was born. What kid isn't fascinated by their own origin story? My mom was in labor all through the night, it began. In those days, the dads sat in the waiting room and smoked cigars through the whole thing,

Mad Men–style, so it wasn't until right after I was born that my dad visited my mom in her hospital room and saw me for the very first time through the glass of that weird baby holding area you've probably seen in old movies. After a nurse pointed out which blob was his, my proud dad headed out to get my mom something to eat. Outside, the sun was just coming up, and maybe because it was so early, there were hardly any cars in the parking lot yet. My dad got into his brand-new red VW Beetle, and somehow, even though he was driving very slowly, and even though there was plenty of space to navigate around it, plowed directly into a lamppost. As a kid, I found this hilarious. As an adult, it occurred to me this was a story of a very young, new dad, who was probably deeply freaked out. But I still found it funny and sweet, and marveled that a half-hour search for his car keys was not also part of the plot. But I could never have predicted how the story of the day of the lamppost would impact my future.

Last year, my friend Jane Levy gave me a reading with an astrologer named Kitty Hatcher as a *Zoey's Extraordinary Playlist* Season One wrap gift. Jane is one of those people who knows who all the best people for everything are. We all need a friend like this. If you're looking for a therapist, a landscaper, a facialist, just ask Jane. I'd never had my chart done before, but because the person was recommended by Jane, I knew she'd be excellent.

Obviously, because it involved keeping track of a piece of paper, no one in my family had seen my birth certificate for decades, and I was worried about not being able to tell Kitty Hatcher the exact time I was born, which I knew was an important detail when getting your astrological chart done. But "the sun was just coming up," as my dad had told me a thousand times, and when I told Kitty that, she said it was good enough for her. Dawn is dawn, even in Honolulu, Hawaii, where I was born. Kitty Hatcher said she'd just do my chart using an estimate of between 5 and 6 A.M., and that would be accurate enough.

When Kitty called me with the results of my reading, I could tell she was excited. She kept saying she'd seen things in my chart that were very rare. She said that in the new year, I'd be given a major position of power. She envisioned me working as a film director, or even running my own television show. She even said I'd been some sort of powerful warrior in a past life. She told me I'd always had some psychic abilities, but that soon I'd be feeling them stronger than ever before, and these abilities were going to help me achieve new levels of success. She told me that the next two years were going to be some of my best, that there were promising planetary convergences in my chart that only happened once in a lifetime, if at all. The fact that all this good fortune had to do with my third house of Taurus being in the fourth sun of Saturn or whatever pretty much went over my head, but the headlines were undeniably fantastic.

I was excited about my now dazzling future and bragged about it to whomever would listen. "I thought you didn't believe in astrology," one of my friends said. I told her that, duh, I believed in it *now* because how could you not when the predictions were so fantastic? It's the same way I "don't believe" in awards unless I'm getting one, and I "don't believe" in reading reviews unless someone tells me they're glowing. And anyway, even if astrology isn't valid, two years from now I'll likely have forgotten that anyone told me I was supposed to be having the best two years of my life because they will just be the two years I've been living in. In fact, I've found that one of the most fun things about getting any kind of reading of the future is that it's usually only deeply important for the one day. I've been to a few psychics over the years, and I couldn't tell you one thing they said to me. Good or bad, it goes right out of my head. I'm sure the details would have stuck with me if I'd written more of them down, but even if I had, I'd probably have lost whatever I'd written them on.

A few weeks after I'd been told that—according to the stars—I was headed for greatness, my stepmother called. She and my dad were moving from their large house in the suburbs to a town house closer to my sister Maggie and her family. "I found a bunch of old notebooks of yours in the attic," she said. "Do you think there's anything in there you might want?" I almost told her to just throw the pile away, since I hadn't used a pile of notebooks for anything since undergrad, and it was doubtful I'd find anything illuminating in the notes I'd taken for my Victorian literature class, but I asked her to send them anyway.

I forgot about our call until a week or so later when a

medium-sized box arrived. In it were some of my notebooks from acting class containing deep thoughts about what my various characters ate for breakfast (Note to actors: this kind of research has never helped me. But in case you're curious, always oatmeal.); some photos of me in bad '90s jeans (so starchy, so puffy, why did you guys bring those back?); and a curious cardboard folder with a black-and-white printed drawing of a regal-looking woman. On the cover below her picture in an ornate font read the words: "Certificate of Birth." Jackpot! Better than a notebook full of oatmeal for sure.

I was born in Honolulu, Hawaii, like I said, at Queen Kapiʻolani hospital, and alongside the sepia-toned queen wearing a large, beaded necklace and a tiara was a similar rendering of the hospital itself, under which was written: Hooulu A Hoola Lahui, which translates to: To Save and Increase the Race. The folder opened like a greeting card, and inside was my name, Lauren Helen, made out in my mom's familiar, loopy script. The rest of the information was typed out on what looked to be an old-fashioned typewriter: my mom and my dad's names, Donna and Lawrence; my weight, 8 pounds 8 ounces; my length, 21 inches; and my time of birth: 12:19 P.M.

Wait.

What?

12:19 P.M.?

12:19 P.M.?

Yes, Reader. 12:19 P.M. A time that is not remotely dawn. A time in which the sun has never, ever risen, except maybe in Iceland. A time that does not resemble 5 A.M. or 6 A.M., and one that is not even a little bit close to the time I gave to Kitty Hatcher, whose mind I blew with my future greatness.

And there, in a flash, the oncoming best two years of my life evaporated before I'd even had a chance to forget they'd been predicted. I waved a sad goodbye to the certainty of my directing career, my awesome psychic abilities, my past life as a brave warrior.

I was disappointed, yes, but it wasn't just the loss of my newly fantastic future that bothered me. If my own father couldn't come close to remembering the time I'd been born, what else was called into question where his memory was concerned? Was anything he'd ever told me in my entire life even remotely reliable? How could I be sure his was the first family on the block to get a TV, for instance? Do ice cream sundae suicides even exist? And who exactly was this "Georgie"? Now I don't know what to believe!

Yet, when confronted by my questions, my father did not seem at all rattled by this new information. "Huh," he said, and shrugged, like it was no big deal. "The way I remember it, the sun was coming up." He said this as if his memory of the matter was not at all disturbed by something as inconsequential as fact. For years, my father told the same story about how a momentous occasion felt to him; the facts had faded over time, maybe because they weren't the most relevant part of the day. Sometimes we polish an experience to make facts line up more closely with feelings or exaggerate moments to make a better dinner party tale. And sometimes, mercifully, details become blurry over time, maybe because the sharp reality is too painful to carry.

When my relationship of almost twelve years ended last year, I went into a sort of shock I'd never experienced before. I'd be doing normal things like driving to the store, or putting in a load of laundry, but also have the sensation of watching myself doing these things from a distance. I felt the energy of having been shot out of a cannon, but somehow the cannonball—me—was also moving in slow motion. It was as if I'd spent a long time watching a movie with ominous background music, not noticing, until it finally swelled to a level I couldn't ignore. And none of these metaphors were quite accurate. I was on the run in a way, determined to always be moving and doing, not giving myself the time to sit and absorb what had happened. It was the middle of the summer, and I rented a house by the beach. Friends and family came to visit, and it was as fun as I imagine a recovery from any injury might be. There was solace in spending time with people I'd missed, but an ache over the circumstances that created that space.

When I returned home to Los Angeles in the fall and people asked me what I'd done for the last few months, I discovered I couldn't remember many of the details. I rented a house, I'd say, and then I'd trail off. One night, I met a friend for dinner. It seemed like we spent a normal amount of time eating and catching up, but when we stood up to leave I realized we'd been there for five hours. During the pandemic, I ordered a smoothie from a little cafe in LA. I picked it up from the makeshift counter set up outside the door, and when I got in the car, I saw there was a small note taped to the top of the cup. It read: "Someday, this will all be a memory." I knew whoever had written the note was thinking about the state of the world and could have had no way of knowing about my comparatively small struggle in it, but this little kindness gave me a moment of hope, a window into the future when the pain of this time would surely have faded a little. I only wondered and worried about how long it was going to take. "Someday" doesn't like to tell you when it plans to arrive.

Maybe the fact that my father remembered it being dawn *was* just as significant as the piece of paper with the bejeweled queen and the correct time. Maybe even more so. Maybe his memory told him the sun was just coming up because having his first child simply felt that way. A new day *is* dawning when a child is born, even if not literally so, and whether that brings panic or joy or a mix of both, it's a moment after which life will never be the same. What does it matter what the clock said? Sometimes, mercifully, without our even asking it to, memory holds hands with fact and helps dull its edges during times when reality is too overwhelming to fully take in a joyous moment, like the birth of a child, or in a darker one, when pain is too great to comprehend, like the loss of a loved one.

Kitty Hatcher redid my chart, and the outlook is still pretty good for the next two years according to her. She thought directing was still a possibility, and she was right it turns out. I'm about to direct an episode of my show *Mighty Ducks: Game Changers,* for Disney+. Some other things looked bright as well, she said, but I forget exactly what. Things will generally be okay, she told me, and that's good enough for me. I got some encouragement that made me feel hopeful—I didn't need to write any of the details down.

The absence of paperwork would thwart my family once again, when one of my Graham cousins tried to do our family tree. We know we are of mainly Irish and maybe also some Scottish descent, but beyond searching our last name, which is common in both places, we can't get very far without birth and death certificates, and we have very few of either. My cousin Heather did get as far as finding the Graham family crest, however, which features a falcon, and a sort of metal-looking belt thing with a big buckle, and our motto: Ne Oublie.

Translated from the Latin, Ne Oublie means: Do Not Forget.

Um.

This information is disheartening in that it tells me it has been predetermined by birth that I will never get any better at not losing my keys, but also comforting in that it teaches me I am not alone, but in fact come from a long line of forgetful ancestors who were so noted for this characteristic that they decided to embrace it and proudly take it up as their mantle. True, it's a pain when I'm trying to leave the house in a hurry, but I'm proud to have come from a family of (possibly) brave warriors who spent countless days driving away with mugs of mead perched atop their chariots, people who've probably spent hours—as I have—searching in vain for their reading glasses, only to eventually discover them on top of their head, where they'd been sitting all along.

Boobs of the '90s

SHORTLY AFTER I moved to Los Angeles from New York in the summer of 1996, I learned a few crucial things: that pale people of Irish descent should not drive convertibles, that all the work I'd done on the plays of Chekhov and Ibsen in my scene study class in the windowless yet magical rehearsal room in Wynn Handman's acting class in the Carnegie Hall building on 57th Street was not going to help me get a job on *Beverly Hills, 90210,* and that—due to it never having occurred to me that it might be necessary to update them— I had possibly left my breasts behind in the previous decade.

I don't remember thinking about my breasts very much—or at all—when I lived in New York. I couldn't tell you what bras I had or even where I got them (Century 21 maybe? Loehmann's?). Kathy, my dear friend and roommate back in Brooklyn, far more well endowed than I, went annually to a special bra place in the East 30s in Manhattan where a professional bra lady would stand behind her in the full-length mirror, adjusting straps and measuring her various dimensions in order to recommend the exact right bra for her, and I remember thinking, who has the time for such a thing? You had to make an actual *appointment*. That's the only New York boobs memory I can conjure—I thought so little about them there that the only story I have is about someone else's.

But after just a few weeks in Los Angeles, I spoke fluent WonderBra, and had purchased my first pair of the rubbery boob blobs no one has ever called anything besides chicken cutlets. These acquisitions didn't seem strange to me at the time, they seemed mandatory, or at least highly recommended. Every audition room I entered was filled with actresses with bigger boobs than mine. I remember thinking I'd better catch up. It felt like everyone knew what sort of boobs they were supposed to have, and weirdly, they also had them. Today, we speak of body positivity, and there is at least an attempt at representing a wider variety of shapes and sizes on-screen, but the boob fashion of the 1990s in Los Angeles seemed to offer actresses only two choices: get them surgically augmented or buy a bra that made it look like you had.

Now, I was mainly auditioning for television, and television in the '90s was largely comprised of half-hour sitcoms, and the most popular sitcom was *Friends*. The friends themselves were all stunning and boobtastic and every other half-hour TV show was trying to mimic their look and their success. Fancy Movie Lady actors may have been going to different auditions with subtler expectations in terms of silhouette. Although I do remember a story going around back then about Frances McDormand pulling her chicken cutlets out at a meeting and tossing them on the table, which was an undeniably bold move, but also told me that even a vanguard like her had at least one day of feeling '90s boobs pressure.

My roommate at the time was Connie Britton. We met in the windowless yet magical Chekhov/Ibsen acting class that wasn't going to get me cast on *90210,* and while she'd eventually become a lifelong friend, we didn't know each other that well yet. We were among the hordes who came from New York every pilot season. Who knew what would happen? We might get cast in something, we might run out of money and go back to New York and start auditioning while waitressing again like we'd seen happen to so many of our friends.

I was driving around town in a rented red Volkswagen Cabriolet with the top down, learning how quickly I sunburned, and Connie had borrowed a vintage gray Volvo with no air-conditioning from a place called Rent-A-Wreck. We bought our first cell phones together and giggled every time we called each other because—besides our agents—we were pretty much the only people we knew in LA, and our New York friends still used the pay phone. These mobiles were ugly and gray and heavy and the only buttons on them were numbers. Bluetooth, GPS, cars with navigational systems, did not yet exist, so to find out where you were going you had to pull over on the shoulder of one of LA's four-lane freeways and manually thumb through the two-thousand-page spiral-bound paper map that was *The Thomas Guide.* You checked your computer—if you even had one—maybe once at the end of the day, and sat staring at it, listening to what felt like an hour and a half of robot static sounds, before the guy finally said, "You've Got Mail." You were lucky if you had a fax machine through which you could print out your audition sides, the pages containing only the scenes in which your character appears, but if you needed to read a whole script you had to drive to your agent's office and pick it up from the bin of envelopes outside the door of the reception area. You knew you were getting somewhere when (if) the agency started messengering things to you rather than have you go to them. Graduating to messenger-level importance was the day we all were hoping for.

Connie and I were staying for free in the house of a friend of hers who was getting a divorce. The friend who'd offered us the house knew we were staying there, but her recently divorced husband did not, so sometimes we'd get a panicked call that the ex was in the neighborhood and we'd have to rush to turn out all the lights and run and hide in the back of the house. We found this hilarious. The house was empty except for two beds and I think one chair and a table we'd sort of move from room to room when needed. There was maybe one pan in the kitchen and the only thing I remember making in it is Rice Krispies Treats, which we'd eat with our hands, too ambitious and dedicated to our craft I suppose to waste even a moment wondering why we had no plates. That was what we considered . . . breakfast, I guess? There was a Subway sandwich shop at the bottom of the street, and we'd walk down there most days and split a tuna sub for lunch and then eat chips and salsa and margaritas at the nearby restaurant Mexicali for dinner, and I was somehow the thinnest I'd ever been. Maybe the Subway tuna salad that would turn out to be the subject of scandal years later, accused of being a "mixture of various concoctions that do not constitute tuna" was to thank. Anyway, Michael Pollan will probably not be writing the foreword to my book *Scientifically Proven Hollywood Miracle Diet* when I publish it, but it'll make millions, I tell you. Millions!

There were other questionable trends that I also didn't question at the time: the need for all miniskirts to be at Calista Flockhart–in–*Ally McBeal* shortness levels, crop tops paired with jeans whose low-rise waistband started maybe a millimeter above the butt crack, and the monthly ritual of getting Brazilian bikini waxes at a salon called Pink Cheeks.

Pink Cheeks was a waxing place on Ventura Boulevard in the Valley rumored to be the top choice of strippers and Playboy Bunnies, which was I guess endorsement enough for everyone. The interior of Pink Cheeks was—no surprise—pink. The chairs were pink velvet and there were Hershey's Kisses in pink candy dishes and everything else in the room was pink and fluffy or lacy or glittery or all of those things. You felt like you were in the bedroom of a 16-year-old aspiring pageant queen who'd swapped her Wham! posters for candy-cotton-colored silk thongs hung on the wall available for purchase. Cindy ran the place, and she was bubbly and huggy and made you feel like you'd stopped by to be served freshly baked cookies and not to pay money to scream out in pain as the most sensitive area on your body was slathered in hot wax and stripped bare.

I haven't been to Pink Cheeks in years and I just looked it up to see if it still exists and it does. Cindy appears to still be running the place, and their website states they now also offer anal bleaching (?), pubic hair tinting/grooming available in a variety of custom colors and shapes (!), and in the FAQs, Cindy cheerfully reports that an unusual/fun fact she's observed over the years is that nearly all of her clients have a small blue mark on their legs or butt that is probably the result of a broken-off portion of pencil lead getting lodged in there at some point when they were younger (?!?!?!?!?!?!?).

Months after we arrived, Connie and I began to acquire mature things like plates and chairs, and each of us booked a few jobs and found one or two more people we could call from our mobile gray bricks. Eventually, I got a guest spot on the sitcom *3rd Rock from the Sun* with John Lithgow and Jane Curtin (giggly student); a recurring part on the Thursday night lead-in to *Friends, Caroline in the City* (kooky airhead); and a small part in a movie starring Patricia Arquette, Ewan McGregor, and Josh Brolin, a thriller called *Nightwatch* (best friend who is also a priest). It occurs to me now that the work I got this first year in Los Angeles was a pretty good indicator of what was to come: mostly comedic roles, an occasional quirky character part, dramatic work once in a while. Connie and I even graduated from being illegal squatters to being actual apartment renters. I got a little one-bedroom on the top floor of a duplex in a building on Orange Street and I thought, for a first-year Californian, how auspicious to be welcomed by citrus. I hired a personal trainer three times a week and started going to spinning classes taught by a woman named Kelly Rockstar who had zero percent body fat and—you guessed it—very large breasts.

I upgraded myself from the Rice Krispies Treat diet too, and I started getting my food delivered in preportioned boxes left on my doorstep every night by a company promising they offered the perfect ratio of fats to carbs to make my body "work more efficiently." Most of the actors I knew at the time were eating their food out of these same boxes. These boxes consisted of a bland protein and a bland vegetable and a tiny bland carb and pretty much everyone ordered them from the same company that was whatever one you read the Friends were currently getting theirs from in the latest issue of *InStyle* magazine. Everyone brought their boxes with them everywhere, transporting them in cooler bags to set, or sometimes even bringing them to dinner parties, and I once went on a date with an actor who brought his box to the restaurant and asked the waiter to heat it up for him and put it on a plate as if he had ordered it there. "What?" he said in response to what must have been a strange look on my face.

"Everyone I know does it." Over time, I didn't stop to ask myself questions like was it okay to bring your own food to a restaurant or why was I on this diet when I was already pretty thin or was Kelly Rockstar her real name or how it might be possible to have zero percent body fat but also have breasts that big.

Then, one day, I got my first boob job. Or rather, my boob blobs got a job. It was a small part in a film for which I had my fake large chicken cutlets to thank. The shoot was out of town, and even though I only had one day of work, they flew me first-class and put me up at the nicest hotel I'd ever stayed in. I'd never been on location before. That night, I was so nervous I hardly slept. The next morning in the makeup chair, I became even more flustered when the makeup artist accidentally used a faulty eyelash curler that chopped a chunk of lashes off my eye—it was not an auspicious start to the day. Worse, after I'd just been told I had plenty of time to get ready, a red-faced assistant director, whose job (among many other things) it is to keep the day running on schedule, appeared in the door of the trailer to say that no, actually, they were ready for a blocking rehearsal, which is where the director and actors work out where we'll be sitting or standing or crossing in a scene so the director of photography and his crew know how to light it—and they were ready for me, NOW.

My wardrobe for the day consisted solely of a (very stuffed) bra and underwear, and I'd been given a thick terry-cloth bathrobe to use as a cover-up. I'd hardly ever been on a movie set, let alone been the day player who might be holding things up on one, so I took off running, barefoot, bathrobe flapping open behind me. This meant that while I arrived on set as quickly as I could, I was sweating and the bottoms of my feet were black from the sidewalk and let's not forget the eyelash amputation I'd recently endured. Heart pounding, I tried to clear my head and focus on rehearsing the scene.

Blocking and rehearsing a scene with two people in bed is like trying to make Twister-type contortions look sexy and natural while also pretending you feel great about doing it. It's awkward. Tilt your face two inches this way and you're blocking your co-star's light, rotate your shoulders two inches that way and the cameraman can't see your face. Rehearsing these moves is technical but also crazily intimate. Have you ever been sitting in a packed theater and dropped something and tried to find it beneath the chair of the stranger next to you while smiling and apologizing? Your head is way too near their lap but you're trying your best to be polite and act like it's normal? Something like that. Plus, only very recently did anyone think it might be a good idea to employ a third party whose job it is to take some of this head-in-a-stranger's-lap awkwardness away by inventing the job of intimacy coordinator. Before then, someone who may or may not have had any experience in such scenes—maybe someone from the wardrobe department—would hover nearby until the director called cut, and then she'd scurry over to cover you with a sheet or fling a bathrobe at you. I could never ever find the sleeves in these bathrobes and rooting around to find them made me panic, which ensured I couldn't find them for even longer.

Recently, I had a scripted kiss with Josh Duhamel's character on an episode of *Mighty Ducks* and I had my first encounter with an intimacy coordinator. It's a family show, and our kiss was described as brief, we were standing up fully clothed and there wasn't much more to it. But I felt kind of guilty that someone had been hired to help coordinate two adults in their 50s share a tongueless peck. So I asked the coordinator what her role on other shows had been, hoping I'd find a problem I needed her expert help in solving. "I'm here to make you comfortable, and ensure there is consent." I cannot tell you how hard I had to bite back my nervous impulse to make a joke. "Consent? Have you *seen* Josh Duhamel? I'd happily . . ." No no no we don't say flippant things in delicate situations, my brain told me just in time. So instead, I said nothing and nodded my head a few times and wandered away and thus ended the coordination of my intimacy. She carried a large bottle of Listerine with her all day with two little cups in separate baggies, which was a thoughtful touch.

Now, maybe actresses like Barkina Plumefessen enjoy strutting around all day ignoring the bathrobe entirely and chatting with everyone, legs akimbo, like they're on a beach in Ibiza. But in my experience no matter who you are these situations are at least mildly awkward and can be confusing to the body. Sometimes you may start to think you are genuinely attracted to your scene partner and sometimes you are, and maybe you even kissed them already the night before outside the Ritz-Carlton, but here, in the scene, you have to pretend it's happening for the first time. This difficulty distinguishing reality from pretend has resulted in some good relationships but many more that were a bad idea and is where the term "showmance" was born. It's a romance born from the intensity and confusion that can occur when you're pretending to be other people. Sometimes you and your co-star will end up together but it's just as likely that when you get back home to reality you'll wonder what you possibly could have seen in each other. This confusion can be even more, er, apparent for men. One male actor I worked with said to me, before a sexy scene, "I apologize if I do, and I apologize if I don't." Ballsy!

Back on set that day after myself and my scene partner and the director had choreographed the scene and rehearsed it a few times, and I had twisted myself into various pretzel shapes for the camera while trying to look cool doing it, the director told everyone to take a short break and he pulled me aside. He smiled and said he was genuinely thrilled to have me in the part, apologized for the morning's rush, and told me the shot he was trying to get was turning out to be more of a puzzle than he'd planned, and he wasn't getting the angle he needed, and he was terribly sorry to ask me this at the last minute, but would I mind taking my bra off in the scene?

I certainly don't wish this upon either of us, Reader, but should we ever get into a fender bender together, I'm a great person to have nearby. In the face of any sort of surprise or trauma, I become very, very calm. This is helpful in that I'm not going to freak out and make an already stressful situation worse, but I'm not sure it's a response that offers a ton of options to the person (me) who is responding to the stress/trauma. That day, I sort of went numb and rather than take a moment to consider how his request made me feel, I remember it being very important to me to act really calm because I wanted to seem professional and also didn't want to hurt the director's feelings. I wish I could tell you I said, Give me a moment to think about it. I wish I could tell you I said I thought we should get my manager or agent on the phone. Or even said, Hell no, Dude, this is why lawyers spend months contractually defining every single body part that will or won't be seen down to the very last detail of whatever the legal language is for "side boob." I wish the next part of the story was about the time I pulled my cutlets out and tossed them boldly on the floor, McDormand-like. I wish I could tell you that was the day I realized that even though I'd only been in LA for a short time, I suddenly became aware of how narrow the definition of what I was expected to look like had become, and that it occurred to me in that moment that if actor, stripper, and Playboy Bunny were different jobs, why were we all supposed to have the same body type? I wish I could tell you that I recognized this situation as inappropriate, a violation of an agreement we'd already spent weeks negotiating.

But I was new. I was intimidated. I was hungry and I was hustling. Also, I was practical. I had done what I was comfortable doing in pursuit of a job, and the number-one thing on my mind was keeping that job. I had padded my bra like I'd padded my résumé. It was just another piece of the costume I was wearing in pursuit of the role of Aspiring Actress, no worse a lie than listing the nonexistent Taos Outdoor Theater on my résumé, where I had supposedly played Rosalind in *As You Like It,* another credit I had come to realize was also not going to help me get on *90210.* Actors are pretenders, and I'm not sure I saw these fabrications as something that took away from the Real Me. The voices questioning the bigger picture I was being sold were in there, brewing, and they'd gather strength over the years, but my first reaction to the director in that moment was a thought resembling, *I can't take my bra off because then he'll know how much fakery is in here and I'll be exposed (literally) for how big (small) my boobs actually are.*

I somehow kept my bra on that day. I didn't so much stand up for myself as I jokingly referenced the nudity clause and said a too-nice, fun-girl-not-wanting-to-make-waves version of "that makes me uncomfortable," and since then have spent most of my career playing affable best friends and talkative single moms whose boobs were not often called on to perform solo whilst uncovered. But I kept my Wonder-Bras in rotation on all my auditions, and my cutlets were always on standby.

Not long ago, I was sitting under an umbrella on Mae Whitman's patio, and she mentioned wanting a new bra for work.

Mae: I like the one I'm wearing, but the lace is itchy.

Me: Well, you should get a bra. That thing you're wearing is not a bra.

Mae: (confused) This bra I'm wearing? This bra is a bra.

Me: (overusing air quotes) That "bra" you're "wearing"
is not a "bra." It's like two triangles of "tissue paper"
held up by a piece of "ribbon." You need, like, "pad-
ding" in there if you want a bra for "work."

One fun thing about having Mae as a friend is that we're
so close that at times I forget we aren't the same age. But then
I'll use too many air quotes or say Phoebe Bridgers when I
really mean to say Phoebe Waller-Bridge, and she'll get a particular look of pity on her face, and it hits me that—oh
yeah—I'm twenty years older than she is, and possibly out of
touch with The Kids Today. That day on her patio, Mae explained to me that most women she knew had stopped using
as much boob fakery in the aughts, and it struck me that extremely short skirts and low-rise jeans were also a thing of
the past, and that once again my boobs had quite possibly
expired. It occurred to me that I hardly ever hear of anyone
who wasn't a Real Housewife getting their breasts surgically
augmented anymore, and that almost none of the other
thirty-year-old actresses I know ever mention the Wonder-
Bra even as a joke, and maybe don't even know of its existence. Certainly, none of them refer to their breasts as "the
girls," as if they had two hard-partying sorority sisters living
inside their shirt. I realized my '90s boobs belonged back in

time with my daily devotion to the Iced Blendeds from The Coffee Bean & Tea Leaf, driving with the top down, and the occasional American Spirit Ultra Light—other things I'd grown out of or left behind long ago. I made coffee at home now, never left the house with an SPF under 45, and hadn't had a single drag of anything in twenty years. I went home that day, cleared the bulkier bras out of their drawers, and when I found some well-worn cutlets in the very back, rather than thinking of replacing them, I threw the pair away.

It also occurred to me that no one got their meals delivered in plastic containers promising efficiency anymore because we'd finally learned what our bodies really needed: GREEN JUICES. Here in the 2000s we have learned the secret: we must constantly be cleansing our systems to rid ourselves of the hideous toxins we've somehow accumulated. The cooler bags with plastic containers of the '90s have now been replaced by cooler bags with recyclable mason jars of green juice and bland green salads with bland raw dressings or the delicious alternative, cooler bags of bland green soups with no dairy no sugar no meat no salt no oil. We've finally got this health thing figured out! I don't know how we made it through the '90s with all those toxins swimming around. I guess it was only due to our attention to bodily efficiency. I'm old enough now to identify these trends partially as a result of science and research, partially one fad simply replacing another. Yet I don't seem to have learned those lessons well enough to be able to resist whatever the newest one is that comes my way. So if you see me out some day wearing a torpedo-shaped bra and downing green powder out of a packet, don't be surprised.

I feel that, in asking these tough questions, I may have taken some of the fun out of boobs and left us all a bit deflated. I don't want the mood to sag here. Let me see if I can perk things up. I'm pretty sure I've learned my lesson now, and I must tell you, that really takes a weight off my chest. Nevertheless, I pledge to continue to do my breast to keep up with the times. Before I go, I just want to give a shoutout to all my friends in Silicon Valley. (I know the difference between Silicon and silicone—it's just comedy, people.) It's true, I don't yet know what shape the boobs of the future will take, but with the help of my fond mammaries of the '90s, I don't think I'll ever again allow them to fall flat. I believe that, thanks to the support of people like Mae in my life, I will stay uplifted, and in the future shall avoid falling into any more booby traps. In conclusion, while I'm not sure what the boobs of the '20s will turn out to be, I am pretty sure that, whether I'm driving, or bra shopping, or acting, I'll never again be caught with my top down. By the way, I never did get a part on *90210,* but I guess that's just tough titties.*

---

* The above paragraph brought to you in partnership with Mae Pity Face™.

Ryan Gosling Cannot Confirm

THIS IS A story about the mysterious world of Hollywood hierarchies, including the time my eyebrows failed an audition for not being famous enough—more on that in a moment. This is not a story about Ryan Gosling doing anything wrong. I have nothing negative whatsoever to say about Ryan Gosling. For one thing, I think he's a fantastic actor. And I don't know him personally, but once, many years ago, I was seeing a band at a small bar in Hollywood (it makes me feel extremely cool to tell you that, but let's be honest, there have been perhaps three times in the last ten years when I have gone to see a band at a bar, or anywhere else), and Ryan was standing outside smoking a cigarette. (Was he? I'm not sure. Was smoking allowed near entrances back then? If so, was this sighting perhaps more than several years ago when smoking was still allowed near entrances, in which case it's maybe once in *twenty* years that I've gone to see a band?) Anyway, what if he wasn't smoking or what if he was but he doesn't want his mom to know because he told her he quit because he doesn't want her to worry? I don't want to get him in trouble because this doesn't really have to do with him in the way you might think. So, let's say he wasn't smoking but rather was being a good son and texting his mom. But if it was twenty years ago, did phones even do that yet? I should really keep a diary.

Anyway, Ryan Gosling looked up briefly from smoking/ texting his mom and gave me the "Hey, we don't know each other but I'm an actor and you're an actor" sort of respectnod, which is less intrusive than a full interaction but friendlier than not interacting at all. This made me like him instantly because he clearly knows about the bylaw that states that it is the job of the more prominent actor who is a stranger to give the less-prominent actor stranger the respectnod. How it is determined who is the more prominent actor and therefore whose job it is to nod first is hard to say, but I don't make the bylaws of respectnodding, I just attempt to follow them. I gave him a respectnod back, and the whole brief exchange made me feel that he was a friendly and nice guy. He also goes to one of my favorite sushi restaurants, which you can find on the corner of Main Street and— Hey! I'm not telling, quit trying to get it out of me, let the man enjoy his albacore belly in peace.

I was doing publicity for *Gilmore Girls: A Year in the Life* for Netflix (no, I didn't get my blue coat back, but the nice people at Warner Bros. bought me a new one, which is red, and no, I won't tell you if I'm team Jess or team Logan and no, Amy hasn't told me any of this, but if I had to guess I think Logan is the father even though it could also be fun if it's the Wookiee, but no matter who the father is I think the baby is a girl whose name is another permutation of Lorelai, I'm going to go with Lola). Around this same time, Ryan Gosling was promoting *La La Land,* and we were both tentatively booked on one of the talk shows that happens in the nighttime, it doesn't matter which one. Both projects were premiering in November, which is a very crowded time for press because the holidays are a popular time for movies to be released, especially ones that have—or hope to have—Oscar buzz. Consequently, all the fanciest people are booked on all the talk shows, and while I, and the television reboot of *Gilmore Girls,* was considered perhaps a little bit fancy, everything in Hollywood is determined by a pecking order whose rules are like the Rules of Respectnodding in that everyone knows they exist, but no one knows what they are or how they work. Sometimes I am the first guest on these shows and sometimes the second, but Ryan Gosling promoting a movie with Oscar buzz was indisputably higher in fanciness according to any law, and so he had been booked as the first.

A few weeks before the show was to tape, I got a call from my publicist, Cheryl. "We might have an issue with the booking of that show that airs in the nighttime," was not exactly what she said. What she did say was: "Ryan Gosling cannot confirm." She went on to explain that Ryan Gosling did not love doing a lot of publicity, which I totally understand, because after years of being asked about what funny pranks go on behind the scenes (very few) and what your costars are really like (either very nice and hardworking, which is a boring truth to tell, or sort of mean/crazy/annoying, which is something we all sign a paper saying is information we'll never share when we join the Screen Actors Guild), it can be hard to drum up material and very stressful to try to be attractive and funny in a few short segments.

Yet what are the options? No one at home wants to be told they should watch a movie or TV show because it's just okay. And even something you've watched that you think was the worst waste of time ever was made by at least a hundred people and some of them had to think it was good and worthy and proudly called their parents to remind them to tune in. Brutal honesty won't make networks and movie studios very happy, and it's certainly not what fans would like to hear. But I understand the inner conflict that having to be both an artist and a salesperson can create, and if I were Ryan Gosling, I'd be Not Confirming all over the place.

It used to be that actors were only expected to do some talk shows and interviews, and pose for some photo shoots here and there where you try to look comfortable while standing tiptoe on one foot on a beanbag chair perched on a diving board. But now people get frustrated if they can't pull up your Instagram account 17 times a day to check on which famous Chris you're currently dating. I can't seem to convince most of the rest of the world that this is not a change for the better. (It's almost as if I'm sending mixed messages, like valuing privacy whilst also being the author of a second book of personal essays.)

Anyway, Ryan was apparently undecided as to what appearances he would be making where. "Good for him," I said to Cheryl.

"But that means you're not confirmed either," Cheryl said.

"No, remember, we confirmed last week?"

"Yes. *We* confirmed last week, but now that Ryan can't confirm this week, they can't confirm you for next week either."

Doing late-night talk shows is one of the extracurricular activities of being an actor I really look forward to. There is a particular type of adrenaline boost that talk shows bring: the combination of enjoyable banter and a live audience that is unique to these appearances. It gives me the thrill of live theater without having to commit to doing eight shows a week. And the stakes felt higher than normal: I felt both pride in what we'd accomplished during *A Year in the Life* and also a wee bit of pressure to do what I could to promote it, so this news made my stomach drop a little.

What followed was an interesting study in Hollywoodery, because the days leading up to this show were sort of about fame and sort of about gender and sort of about casting, and sort of about running out of time and spectacularly—although briefly—about Cher.

Hierarchies exist in every industry, otherwise every person at your company would get the corner office. But there seem to be an endless number of Hollywood hierarchies that no one tells you about or admits to, and the only way you'd know they exist is by experiencing them, and no matter how many years I've been in this business, I keep discovering new ones.

During the second year of *Gilmore Girls,* I was offered the Louis Vuitton discount, which I didn't know existed at the time, which is, as you might guess, a discount at Louis Vuitton. Ooh, that's a tough one to get, my publicist told me, which is the way I learned that *other* discount lists like it existed. Very short list, she told me. Madonna is on that list. I was thrilled to be on that list, but it was also somewhat lost on me at the time. Even though I was making a good salary and had finally landed on a show that seemed like it was going to last for a while, these were realities that hadn't yet sunk in, like being able to afford things at Louis Vuitton, especially with a discount. My bank balance might recently have been promoted, but my brain was still a waitress back in Brooklyn, struggling to make enough tips to pay the rent. Today there isn't a suitcase in sight I wouldn't welcome home from Louis Vuitton because I am older and think of things like collecting matching luggage sets to pass down to my nieces even though they probably won't care about such things because by the time they're old enough to travel solo they'll probably have decided to eschew clothing in favor of sustainable onesies that double as sleeping bags, but still.

I remember buying a light blue suede blazer sort of thing there that fastened with a large blue suede butterfly-shaped button, and it was such a bold piece and so fancy, and I had no idea what I'd do if it got dirty. Do you dry-clean suede? Send it to a suede specialist? Have it airlifted to an atelier in France? These concerns left it mocking me from the back of my closet. Then Michelle Pfeiffer appeared on the cover of *InStyle* magazine in it, and for one or maybe all of these reasons I hardly ever wore it. But I did buy a few purses, and every time I shopped there they were really nice to me. However, I was not offered the LV discount the next year and somehow, without being told, I knew that this was a "don't call us, we'll call you" situation and that was the end of that. This was one of the first times I learned about a hierarchy too late to make use of my knowledge, but it wouldn't be the last.

When I was starting out and on one of the many half-hour shows I did that ended up getting canceled in the middle of its first season, a producer came to set and asked me if I would be willing to dye my hair. I'm sure I was thrilled to be singled out for any reason, thrilled to think that executives were discussing anything about me, even if it was just how many highlights I'd be needing. But I tried to seem serious actress-y and asked him what he had in mind, what kind of change he was going for, how he envisioned the character.

"It doesn't really matter," he told me, waving his hand in the air. "We just want to make sure people can tell you and Blah-blah apart." When I tell you that Blah-blah and I looked nothing alike—please take my word for it. It would have been like saying you wanted me to dye my hair so that people wouldn't confuse me with Chrissy Teigen. In fact, let's just say it *was* Chrissy Teigen. "We don't want the audience to be confused about whether you're you or you're Chrissy Tei-gen, so we're wondering if lighter hair might help." It had nothing to do with the character at all, it was more about how things looked. I shouldn't have been surprised by yet another example of how this was an industry in which visu-als trumped everything, but I was still new. I guess the hier-archy issue here was that it was I, and not the other actress, who was asked to make the adjustment. Even being asked to make an adjustment at all was evidence of where I stood, importance-wise, as I learned years later on a pilot when the director simply said: "How do you want to wear your hair?"

I learned quickly that at awards shows, the most famous people were courted by the best designers, and the rest of us got what gowns were left over, which was obviously still in-credible, and there was often a fun surprise on the actual day when someone who'd been holding several possibilities finally made her choice and a dress was "released." What took me longer to understand was that the arrival times at these shows and the parties that followed them had a pecking order as well.

The *Vanity Fair* party is held right after the Oscars have been given out and is a tough ticket to get. Many of the photos from the party are subsequently published in the magazine or online, and therefore they can't have Denzel Washington getting there at the same time as Michelle Wil-liams because the photographers want solo photos of every-one, and if all the famous people arrived at once there would be a backlog of famous people standing around waiting to have their picture taken rather than being photographed and whisked through the line to get to their martini, and maybe some of them would get frustrated and decide to skip the line altogether in order to get to their martini, which would be a bummer for *Vanity Fair,* so each ticket comes with a time. Actually, Denzel and Michelle can probably get there whenever they want, but people who aren't them are given an arrival time, as I learned the first time I was invited. "Ooh, that's a good time," my publicist told me, which is how I also learned there were times that were considered bad times. I'm guessing being invited either so early that all your makeup has slid off your face by the time the party is in full swing or so late that Denzel and Michelle have long ago moved on to the other parties are the "bad" slots.

The best hair and makeup people get booked up as well, and in some cases are put on hold waiting for a special client. I had a makeup artist whom I loved working with tell me she probably wouldn't be seeing me for a while because Nicole Kidman had booked her for the year. FOR THE WHOLE YEAR. Like how would that even work? Is she on call, like some sort of ER doctor? Who pays for her to be taken off the market? It doesn't matter exactly, but when you lose a makeup artist or any other artist to someone more important than you, it can't help but feel like you've been a little bit broken up with by a guy who traded up to a hotter girl.

Back to the show that airs at some point after the evening news: once Ryan Gosling could not confirm, they couldn't confirm me because they weren't sure if they could come up with an actor of Ryan's status who was also a guy to replace him. This was communicated in more vague language than that, but it became clear that having two female guests, no matter who they were, was not an option. You may think to yourself: but all these shows are hosted by men, so why would you need another man, even for the visual? The answer is, I don't know. As the night of the booking approached, various names were tossed around, but for whatever reason the evening program wasn't sure they were a "fit." Various male names were floated and discarded, basically for not being famous enough and/or not having a movie with Oscar buzz, but still it seemed in comparison to these discards I wasn't famous enough to go first and have the less famous guys whom they were discarding go second. Again, no one exactly said this.

Then Cher's name came up, and for one glorious moment, it seemed possible that Cher might be the lead guest, which would make it okay for me to go second. This was thrilling because of the thought of getting to sit next to Cher, but also an interesting lesson in hierarchy because not only did Cher not have a movie with Oscar buzz, I don't think she had anything she was promoting, and also she's obviously a woman, but no one cared, so excited were they by the possibility of having Cher on the show, and thusly I learned that there are exceptions to the Hollywood bylaws, and one of them just says CHER. So, there are rules as clearly stated in the bylaws, but some of those rules don't apply to Ryan Gosling, and even fewer of them apply to Cher and maybe that's just good old democracy. Or gerrymandering, I'm not sure which.

I've learned a great deal over the years, but who has power in this business and why remains mysterious to me. So much of it is so subtle and unspoken, and those in power aren't always transparent about how they got there. Strides have been made I guess, although I don't see that many more women than I used to working as directors or producers or even crew members. And even though I've been doing this for a while now, I still have to psych myself up to ask for things, and I still worry about being polite and confirming in a timely manner, whereas other people are rightly taking care of themselves as artists and being authentic and not try-ing to sell a car unless they really believe in it. I try to practice gratitude for all the opportunities I've had, but sometimes having good manners doesn't translate to getting results, which leads me to my eyebrows and their audition.

A friend told me about a fantastic eyebrow grooming place but warned me it was tough to get an appointment, especially since they did their bookings largely through Insta-gram, which I'm not on. "Have your publicist call and tell them who you are," my friend advised. That seemed unnec-essary to me. It's not that I've never asked someone to call to book a restaurant or something on my behalf, but I thought, really? I need extra muscle for an eyebrow appointment? Surely my eyebrows could get their own table. So, I used the ancient art of the telephone to leave the eyebrow masters a message, and confusingly was sent a very elaborate question-naire via email in return.

My college application asked me fewer questions than

the eyebrow document did. There were questions about medical history, and questions about prior brow experiences, and a confusing section that inquired as to my "expectations." I answered them all, including a section where I admitted to having my brows microbladed many years before. Microblading is like a mild version of a tattoo. It fades over time and in a very subtle way makes your eyebrows look a bit thicker, saving me time in the makeup chair in the morning.

I sent my brow application in and wondered briefly if I should have applied to a safety school. A few days later, a somewhat stern response came my way. The brow artist to whom I was applying was concerned about my past microblading, as she did not like being constrained by "other people's work," and could I please send in a photo of my brows?

I wish I'd quit right there or at least given up on handling this myself and had my publicist call. I don't like taking pictures, and I'm the only person in the world who takes a total of maybe three selfies a year, and in general I think it's not a good idea to send photos to strangers. But my embarrassment had taken on an embarrassment of its own, and more than I dreaded a photo of Lorelai's eyebrows ending up on the Internet, I wanted this job for my brows. I took ten hundred photos of myself and hours later picked what I thought was a winner.

In the end, Ryan Gosling did not end up doing the show that airs late at night even though it's filmed at around 4 in the afternoon, and neither did I. The problem with not confirming is that talk shows rely on having guests and at a certain point they have to bump you for someone they can count on. And as a guest, you don't want to be known for saying yes and then pulling out at the last minute. Eventually, the waiting on both ends became too much, and Cheryl was concerned I'd lose the booking altogether, so I withdrew and did other shows instead and have since been back to all the shows of the eveningtimes and no hard feelings toward anyone. Two other people whose names had never even come up did the show that night. The first guest was a man, and the second guest was a woman, and—sadly for all of us—neither of them were Cher. And my eyebrows never even got a callback. They left Hollywood to work at a small nightclub in the Poconos where you can probably get a table any night, as long as you call to confirm.

R.I.P. Barneys New York

Shortly after I graduated from Barnard College in the spring of 1988, I got my first New York City apartment. I ran into the fraternal twin of a guy I'd briefly dated while looking up listings in the Columbia University housing office, and based solely on this coincidence we decided to become roommates. We found a two-bedroom walk-up in a brownstone on 21st Street and 7th Avenue that had no living room. The front door opened onto a tiny kitchen, which led to two bedrooms that each faced an air shaft. There was one bathroom whose door was inexplicably three stairs up from the kitchen floor, so technically, one would ascend to the bathroom, and the word "ascend" was the only remotely fancy thing about the place.

This was back during a time when we believed that fats and not carbs were the enemy, and while I think we had an oven, the only thing I remember anyone cooking in there was when my roommate's girlfriend—an aspiring model—made her daily meal comprised of flour and water and maybe a little bit of sugar, which she would mix in a bowl and nuke in the microwave until it rose into a sort of spongy bread porridge, which she had to eat right away or it would collapse into a gluey gray puddle. She was very thin.

I was excited to have my first grown-up place—humble though it was—and I wanted to make it feel homey. My decorating experience was limited to the time I tacked a poster of Monet's *Water Lilies* to my senior-year dorm room wall, but that wasn't going to deter me. Inspired by extensive research involving maybe three issues of *Martha Stewart Living* magazine, I bought an oversized rooster stencil and began to sponge-paint a string of them, nose to tail, following each other around the border of the ceiling. Halfway through my project, I realized that all the sponge-painted roosters in the world weren't going to turn this crummy apartment into a preppy Connecticut cottage, plus my arm hurt, and I stopped. Six and a half roosters did not a stencil border feature make, but I didn't really have time for more sponge crafts anyway. I needed a job.

I mean, I *had* a job, as a waitress at the comedy club the Improv, on 44th Street near Ninth Avenue in Hell's Kitchen. I needed *another* job, a more reliable one. Weekend shifts at the Improv were the most lucrative and therefore the hardest to come by, especially if you were new, as I was, but even the servers with seniority were subject to the bizarre whims and temper of our boss. If you put the wrong date on your check or forgot a customer's ketchup or dropped a drink, she'd take a shift away. Sometimes she'd lose track of how many of us she'd punished, and she'd find herself short-staffed. The reason so many actors start out as waiters is that working at night leaves the days free for all the auditions you're supposedly busy having. But the only auditions I could get without an agent or a union membership were open calls. I'd pore over the pages of the casting trade paper *Backstage,* and stand in line for hours for the chance to do a few lines of a monologue or a few bars of a song before the inevitable "Next" or "Thank you." And even those were rare.

Adding to that uncertainty, the comedy scene was starting to wane a bit in the late '80s. Some nights the club was full, other nights not. *Seinfeld,* the TV show, would air later that year, but Jerry himself was already popular. He'd also already left New York and moved to Los Angeles. It was rumored that he still stopped by the Improv to try out new material when he was in town, but he never showed up during any of my shifts. I remember Ray Romano performing there a few times, then he too left to do his TV show on the West Coast. What remained in New York City were the few headliners who had not flocked to LA, lured by sitcom pilots and writing deals, and those just starting out. One of my favorite comics, Dave Attell, went on to become a successful writer and performer, but back then he worked the door taking tickets for the privilege of going on last every night.

One of the regular comics at the Improv, a handsome and funny guy named Marty Rackham, told me he'd heard I was looking for work and he had a friend who worked at Barneys New York, a clothing store near my apartment on 7th Avenue that I'd never gone into because I'd passed the entrance once right as someone was exiting and the smell that wafted onto the street told me I couldn't afford anything in there. But somehow, through Marty and his friend, I got an interview, and to my surprise, a few weeks later, I was hired to work on the third floor, home to the Barneys private label and a few other designers that made upscale classics for the stylish working woman.

The first thing they taught us in our sales associate training was never to judge the clients by what they were wearing, because very rich people didn't always dress like they were very rich. It had never occurred to me that there was a category of rich people who were so rich that they didn't care if they looked rich, which to me defeated the purpose of being rich, but what did I know. I wore puffy black Reebok high-top sneakers with most outfits, and I considered a nice dinner out a grilled cheese with tomato from the diner on our corner. I knew nothing. If you were a customer who asked me back then if the blouse you were trying on was too see-through for your Manhattan law office and I assured you it was not, I apologize. I had no idea

what people in offices wore or what people in offices did
and I had no office skills whatsoever; I wrote my college
thesis on a word processor and corrected it with Wite-Out,
and the sheerest shirt I owned was a cotton button-down
from the Gap.

In our training they also taught us that shoplifting was
bad. I felt like everyone probably knew that already, but they
put a next-level fear in all of us. Someone had gotten fired for
taking home a sample lipstick from the cosmetic counter.
Even if they'd done so accidentally, it didn't matter, they told
us. There was a zero-tolerance policy, and our bags and
purses would be checked every time we entered or exited the
store.

Back in seventh grade, my friend Esmenk Porcupine (not
surprisingly not her real name) and I spent countless after-
noons thumbing through *Tiger Beat* magazines at the popular
preteen hangout spot, the People's Drug in Arlington, Virginia. Price tags then were pretty much just stickers, and one
day Esmenk showed me how easy (and fun!) it was to switch
the price tag of, say, a pair of men's tube socks with the fashion scarves everyone wore then, which tied at both ends and
had that metallic thread running through them. I guess we
knew price-tag switching was wrong, since when we did it
we tried to make sure no one saw us do it, but at the time I
was simply blown away by my friend Esmenk's incredible
ability to make the world make sense for her. Esmenk was
allowed to stay up to watch *Saturday Night Live*. Esmenk's
parents had the playbill from the Broadway production of

Oh! Calcutta!, whose cover featured a dozen or so half-naked people. On the weekends they'd let us sleep outside in a tent in their backyard and would hardly ever check on us, which we used as an opportunity to climb over the fence in her backyard and run down the hill to buy snacks at 7-Eleven. Esmenk smoked pot but was also a cheerleader who got good grades. Esmenk was the most sophisticated person I knew, and time spent with her was the closest I'd ever come to a life of crime. But by the time I got hired to work at Barneys, price tags had evolved from their sticker days, and anyway I was more worried about what I would wear to work at a chic place like Barneys than I was about accidentally pocketing a lipstick.

My shifts at Barneys started at 8 A.M. and ended around 3 P.M., at which point I'd change into my stretchy black pants and puffy Reebok high-tops and race to get to the Improv and work until one or two in the morning and come home and do it all again the next day. Even working this many hours, I was just scraping by. I had student debt I was trying to pay off. On my days off, I'd paw through the racks of the discount clothing stores on 8th Street to try to look like someone qualified to advise anyone on what to buy at Barneys. Thankfully, we were sometimes allowed to borrow a blazer or a sweater from the floor in order to "model" them for the customers.

Julia Roberts walked through our floor one day, the first famous person I'd ever seen in real life. I imagined going over to her discreetly and letting her know, in a dignified voice, that I too was an actress, and asking her if she had any advice for me. We'd hit it off immediately and she would tell me I was "going to make it," she was certain of it. Then we'd giggle as we reenacted the scene with the sales associates from *Pretty Woman* where I was snooty, and Julia Roberts told me I'd made "a big mistake," except Don't Bother the Famous People was another one of Barneys' strict policies and that movie hadn't been made yet. Later that year I saw Demi Moore, who was being given a private tour of the Mattel Toy Fair, where I'd been hired part-time to demonstrate the Uno card game. These two sightings taught me that famous people are always much tinier and even more depressingly beautiful in person, and it seemed impossible that I'd ever go from demonstrating a family card game or recommending an appropriate level of workplace blouse sheerness to becoming one of them.

A small relief in this daily grind was that Barneys was just a few blocks from my apartment, and on my lunch hour, which I'm pretty sure was only a half hour, I could walk back home and take a break to wonder if my career would be going better if I ate more of the microwave-model porridge. On one such day, I came home and flopped on my bed for a minute, got up after a bit, and on my way to ascend to the bathroom I caught myself in the mirror wearing a five-hundred-dollar black cashmere Ralph Lauren cardigan that I had borrowed from the floor. With no one there to hear me but six and a half sponge-painted roosters, I gasped out loud.

Somehow I had walked off the third floor, down the circular stairs past the second floor, through the accessories and makeup counter of the main floor, and entered the employee checkpoint, passing the guard near the exit who never failed to examine our bags whether we were entering or exiting, and no one, including me, had noticed that I was wearing something different from what I had arrived in. That day, frozen in the middle of my not–living room, I experienced what I can only describe as a panic attack. I couldn't think straight. So haunted was I by my employee training and the story of the sample lipstick that I feared trying and failing to explain myself more than any other option. What if they didn't believe I'd taken the sweater home unintentionally? I couldn't afford to get fired. Thusly, I decided it made the most sense to take the sweater off and hide it in my closet and return to work as if nothing unusual had happened. In other words, so panicked was I to be considered a shoplifter that my solution was to shoplift. I returned to the floor that day, without the sweater, half expecting to be met by law enforcement. For days to come I dwelled in a state of blinding guilt and anxiety. But somehow, no one ever said anything.

As the months dragged on, I realized I had envisioned my life as an actress in New York City as some sort of black-and-white Katharine Hepburn movie in which I'd be rushing from audition to audition alongside the other hoofers and chorines wearing attractive belted leotards and character shoes. These movies had taught me that one day a grizzled, embittered director would experience a moment of softness and take note of my exceptional spunk and I'd join the ensemble in the back row of the musical, waiting until that one night where I was called upon to go on for the leading lady, who'd sprained an ankle, and thusly I'd become The Talk of the Town.

Instead, there had only been a handful of times where I'd managed to take a day off to wait in line for hours at open calls for something I wasn't remotely right for to be performed at a regional theater I'd never heard of. My days and nights were indistinguishable, unremarkable, and just plain tiring. One day I realized with a shock that I'd been at it for over a year. I wondered how many more years could slip by this way. I'd sent hundreds of manila envelopes out containing my headshot and heavily padded résumé to every agency in town, but I wasn't any closer to getting an agent or becoming a union member. I started thinking maybe I needed to make a new plan.

I had a friend who'd been given a scholarship to an MFA program, and he encouraged me to audition for The League, a consortium of schools that all came into Manhattan over the same weekend once a year to see prospective MFA candidates. Most of the training programs were connected to universities in other states. As far back as I could remember, I'd dreamed of making it in New York City. The prospect of leaving New York in order to make it in New York felt like twisted logic, but eventually, that's what I did when I got a scholarship to the MFA Acting Program at Southern Methodist University. My stolen black sweater and I left Manhattan for Dallas, Texas.

Three years later, as a result of the showcase held by my grad school back in Manhattan, I got what I'd left town hoping for: an agent. That year, I got a Cascade dishwashing detergent commercial and for one day I played an assistant who was helping Susan Lucci's Erica Kane stage a fashion show on the daytime drama *All My Children*. The next year, I was a bride in an AT&T commercial, and a bridesmaid in a Hertz commercial. Finally, I got a play at a regional theater in New Jersey, a job that meant I couldn't work retail during the day or be a waitress at night anymore. That spring, after I booked a half-hour pilot in LA, my hardly-worn black sweater and I were on the move to the West Coast. Much was unfamiliar to me there, but it was oddly comforting to drive through Beverly Hills and see a familiar facade with its trademark red awning: a brand-new West Coast branch of Barneys New York. It was a touchstone in a way, a concrete reminder that I'd graduated from sponge painting and puffy sneakers. I'd once worked there, but now I shopped there. I got a few more guest spots and booked a role as a series regular on a half-hour sitcom starring Molly Ringwald, Jenna Elfman, and Ron Livingston. My manager, John, would take me to lunch on the patio of Fred's restaurant on the top floor at Barneys to celebrate these bookings. He always seemed to know everyone and he'd shake hands and introduce me around and I felt pleased and proud to be a working actor. The day I was nominated for a Golden Globe Award I went to Barneys to buy myself my first fancy handbag. It was floppy and orange with hardware so heavy it made my shoulders sore, but it was the "it" bag of the moment. Over the years I shopped there frequently enough to have my own "shoe guy," a salesman who'd set the most popular styles aside for me in my size. But there was always a part of me that was surprised when no one asked me if the blouse they were wearing seemed too sheer for the office. I never entered the building without remembering what it felt like to work there.

One day, I was wandering in the Barneys LA perfume department when someone tapped me on the shoulder. I turned to see a burly man wearing a security badge and my stomach did a little flip. I was momentarily transported back to my not–living room, wearing my not-purchased black cashmere sweater, and my face went hot. Was this the day I'd finally be condemned, revealed as a dweller in the underworld of slippery price-tag-sticker ethics? Had someone been spending years in a basement somewhere poring over vintage Barneys New York security footage, hoping to expose a member of the cast of *Townies*?

The man explained that he worked for Barneys security, and he wanted me to know there were a bunch of paparazzi outside, and that while the store had a strict physical boundary beyond which photographers weren't allowed, for my safety and as a courtesy he would be happy to escort me to the valet and stay with me until I got in my car. The idea that I needed protection against swarms of photographers was thrillingly novel, and I'd been on enough TV shows at the time that I'd occasionally be recognized when I was out, but I had to ask him: surely they hadn't descended on the store in the hopes of catching a glimpse of a recurring character from *Caroline in the City*? He very politely managed not to make me feel insignificant while acknowledging that Gwen Stefani was also in the store.

I shopped a little more but mainly tried not to look as though I was lurking in hopes of catching a glimpse of Gwen (I didn't see her), and when I was finally ready to leave, I took a deep breath and nodded to the guard, and we walked toward the exit. The kind security man walked a few paces ahead of me with a purposeful stride, both shielding me and clearly signaling I was someone who needed shielding. I walked stiffly but with dignity, Julia Roberts–like. Outside, across from the valet stand, dozens of paparazzi were lined up shoulder to shoulder behind a thick hedge, their camera lenses massive and menacing. I handed the valet the ticket for my car and waited for the onslaught of blinding flashes to pop in my face.

Friends, there was no pop. That's right, nary a photo was taken. Not one of them recognized me, or if anyone did, they didn't care. The security man maintained his dignified stance although he seemed confused as I blushed with embarrassment. As I remember it, the wait for my car was approximately eleven-two hours. But he stayed by my side anyway and kindly opened the car door for me when it arrived.

My dear friend Kathy claims I let her borrow the Ralph Lauren sweater once or twice but remembers me staying up waiting for it to come home as if it were a teenager with a brand-new driver's license. I personally never wore it more than a few times. Eventually, I realized I was never going to feel good about wearing it. And the floppy orange Golden Globe celebration bag I'd bought—a trendy shape, a bright color, a choice made during a time I was trying too hard to fit into the role of whatever I thought celebrities were supposed to be—didn't feel right anymore either. I gave them both away.

My sister and I started worrying about Barneys a few years back when on our way up the stairs suddenly every garment we passed was a tie-dyed parachute pant with fringe on it or something with similarly confusing elements. Who wears this stuff? we began asking each other with alarming frequency. Whenever I was back in New York, we had a standing date to shop and brunch at Barneys. We always ordered the salmon salad and Estelle's chicken soup, described on the menu as "Grandma's recipe to cure colds and stay thin." At Christmastime, we'd model sunglasses for one another and then buy each other a pair as a gift, a far more festive exchange somehow than just buying them for ourselves.

It's strange to have feelings for an institution, especially one that can't possibly have feelings for me. Barneys doesn't know it provided the background for so many stages of my life. I was there at the beginning, and I was there at the end, when Gucci loafers went on sale half price for probably the first and last time ever in Gucci history. At that very sale, only a day or two before the doors would close permanently, I bought a small, black YSL crossbody bag—my years spent roaming the aisles there had taught me a few things, and I was no longer lured by floppy orange trends. Barneys' closing left behind a brick-and-mortar-sized hole in my heart, and even though there are hundreds of other brunch spots in New York City, my sister and I still haven't found one that feels as much like our place as Fred's did. We've tried to move on and find a new one, but it always feels like a big mistake.

Big.

Huge.

As a younger person, I don't remember having feelings for a new building going up, but as a less young person, it affects me now when one is destroyed or deserted. Even if it's a place I took for granted: if the dry cleaners on the corner can suddenly shutter, what else can't be counted on to stay the same, to reassure me there is stability—if not in my life, then at least on my block? I feel like I've spent so much of my time as a grown-up figuring out who and what my daily people and places are: these little connections become routine, reliable, until the day when one of them moves locations or a business closes entirely, and your routine has to change. The shift is small and yet a shock to the system, a momentary inconvenience but also a reminder that impermanence looms, and nothing—and no one—lives forever. I don't feel old enough to have worked somewhere as a young girl that my nieces and nephews, now very young, may never have heard of. Not unless they become fashion historians, or vintage floppy bag collectors, or if they someday read their Aunt Lala's book.

But I've Played One on TV

DURING THE FIRST year I moved to Los Angeles, in the early fall of 1996, I mostly spent my days in the car, driving across town from one audition to another. My first car in LA was a truly terrible car—a dented '91 lime-green Honda Civic—but it was the first car I had paid for myself, in wadded-up tip cash from a summer waitressing job in Chicago, so I was perfectly proud to drive it. It wasn't extremely old, but it had been parked outside and was corroded by the salty streets of brutal Midwestern winters. The frame was so rusty in places that there was a spot on the driver's side where you could see through to the ground below. "Just like Fred Flintstone's car!" I'd brag to my friends. I didn't care. I'd grown up on a steady diet of terrible hand-me-down cars. I knew how to work with them. We understood each other and they served me well. No one in my family cared about cars. "A car is just a piece of transportation," my dad was fond of saying. Once, on a 21-hour drive back to Virginia from summer stock in Michigan, the steering wheel column of the giant blue boat that was my used Oldsmobile station wagon started to expel a thin stream of smoke, and rather than pull over to see what the problem was, I decided it would be wiser not to stop at all for the rest of the way. Smoke continued to trickle out of the steering wheel for the remaining four hours of my drive, and after I pulled into our garage, the car died, never to start again, and was towed away for scrap. But in my mind, I had triumphed as a Terrible Car Whisperer once again, and all that mattered was we'd made it.

In LA, the standards were different. Car equaled place in society in a way I'd never encountered in New York. In LA I quickly learned that people didn't see my holey car as a symbol of my ability to carry a tray, but instead viewed it as an object of pity. People seemed to relate to one another according to what level car they had. I was stuck in traffic near the Hollywood Bowl once and a guy in a beat-up pickup truck leaned out of his window and shouted to me: "Hey, we're both driving lemons. We should hang out."

One sunny LA day I was in my terrible car with my then boyfriend, on our way to lunch. I was driving, and as we pulled up to a red light he glanced over to the next lane and said, "I think someone wants a word with you." I leaned forward to look out the passenger-side window, and there, in a fancy vintage convertible that looked like it was the work of some tortured, long-dead European genius, was Jay Leno.

"Your left taillight is out," Jay Leno said. The host of *The Tonight Show with Jay Leno,* Jay Leno!

"Why, thank you, Jay Leno!" I gushed back at him like a freak.

For weeks, it was the only story I told. I called home. I called friends in New York. "Isn't that the *craziest* coincidence?" I squealed to everyone. This occurrence was of course thrilling on its own, but it also felt like a sign. Or rather, I wanted it to be a sign, so I made it into one. When you're a struggling actor waiting for the phone to ring it's hard to not take every ringless day personally, so you look elsewhere for validation. There was the casting person who said I reminded her of Elizabeth McGovern and told me, "We're due for a new one." At the time, I was thrilled by this information, although now it occurs to me that we actors are just so many pieces of steaks being ordered at a fancy restaurant, eaten one day and then ordered again the next day by the same diner hoping for a steak both just as good and yet indistinguishable from yesterday's steak (apologies for this meaty metaphor). There was the landlord I rented from who told me Jennifer Jason Leigh had once rented the same apartment and that probably meant the place was lucky. And now a random encounter with Jay Leno? Signs, everywhere!

Most important, I thought, I now had a story to tell to Jay Leno if ever I was booked on *The Tonight Show with Jay Leno,* which had to mean I would someday be on *The Tonight Show with Jay Leno,* didn't it? What kind of cruel world would this be if Jay Leno told me that my taillight was out if I'm not going to someday go on the show and talk about how sweet that was of him all those years ago, and wasn't Hollywood a magical place where such things happened, and look at me now? If it wasn't a sign, then this story was destined to be retold at dinner parties until over time my friends would whisper behind my back, Oh god, not the Jay Leno at the stoplight story again, lucky for her she makes great tips at that restaurant where she still works.

But a few years later, it happened, and I was asked to appear on *The Tonight Show* for the first time. I had been a guest on the local Los Angeles morning news, the daytime *Donny & Marie* show, and the local morning show *KTLA Morning News.* At this point, *Gilmore Girls* was airing its second season—we weren't a hit exactly, we never really were in terms of ratings, but instead spent seven years slipping quietly under the radar, fueled by positive press and our devoted fans. But the show had generated enough buzz by then that I was deemed "bookable" and this was my first late-night appearance. There, in the dressing room with my name thrillingly on the door, a hairstylist wielded a giant-barrel curling iron while a makeup artist glued eyelashes onto my eyelashes and a stylist steamed borrowed dresses. I was wearing a bathrobe the stylist brought with nothing on underneath, which she'd advised me to do to ensure that whichever dress we chose wouldn't reveal an unsightly indentation left by a bra strap or a line from the seam of my jeans. That anyone would think of this was just one of the many small but uniquely Hollywood details that were completely new to me.

It must have been fairly early in Jay Leno's tenure as host, because among the many people who knocked on my dressing room door that night—a junior producer asking me to sign some paperwork, the sound man wondering if I was ready to be wired, my agent wishing me luck and telling me he'd come back when I was dressed—was also a preppy intern pushing a drinks cart, a sort of minibar on wheels from which he offered to mix you anything you could think of. "That's a holdover from the Carson days," the experienced hair person told us after he passed by. "I hear Jay doesn't like it." I didn't know it then, but I'd be back on the show a few more times before Jay retired, and I never saw the drinks cart again. Not every talk show host likes a Sinatra-level imbiber, I guess.

After I had squozen myself into my outfit and been zipped up—with the help of the stylist pulling at the zipper with both hands and my own two hands squeezing my ribs together, Scarlett O'Hara style—the segment producer knocked on the door. I'd only spoken to her on the phone during my preinterview, and in person she was energetic, blond, and friendly. A preinterview is where a producer asks you questions with the goal of finding stories that would be fun for the audience to hear. Hopefully you come armed with some anecdotes you've been dying to tell. "Keep a talk show notebook," she'd advised, and it's something I still do to this day. After the call, the producer reviews the material with the other producers and usually also the host, and together they determine which of my hopefully hilarious childhood traumas or hopefully hilarious bad audition stories seem most hilarious. If you're someone already well known, the segment producer will have done some research into your last project, your love life, a magazine article they read about you, and ask related questions. "So, Flavina, I read somewhere that you once ate nothing but chocolate for three whole days! You're so nutty! Tell us more about that!" In today's world, they might look at your social media: "So, Flavina, you were really throwing shade at Smarfus on IG over her recent breakup with Grilld Cheez? Tell us more about that!" Some segment producers will give you general insights into what works best for their host. The segment producer on *Letterman* told me Dave didn't like when guests spoke to the audience. Dave's feeling was that when a guest kept switching back and forth between talking to him and talking to them, it kind of broke concentration with both and that it made for better television—and better comedy— to mostly maintain eye contact with him, which is a tip I took with me to every show after that. Some hosts drop by the dressing room to say hello (Conan, Leno), some don't (Letterman, Ellen, unless it's around Halloween and she's hiding in your dressing room in order to scare the bejeezus out of you). Some actors make it all up. Some actors, I'd later learn, have writers from their show write them completely fabricated funny stories.

But I didn't know any of that then. That night, in the *Tonight Show* dressing room, I was very green and all I knew was that it was hard to breathe when your ribs are being squozen, and I had one story guaranteed to not be a total disaster that I'd waited for years hoping to use. The producer went over the order of what stories went where: I'd go out, Jay would say hello, tell people it was my first appearance, talk a little about my background and the budding success of *Gilmore Girls,* etc. Then we'd get to the car story.

"Oh! And we all thought it would be funny if you said the car was a Pacer," she said brightly.

"Oh, really?" I said, confused. "But it wasn't a Pacer. It was a Honda."

"I know, but don't you think Pacers are just *funnier?*"

"I—wait—so you mean, just *make it up?*"

This seems like a quaint moment from ye olden times now, but as a kid who was allowed to stay up late for only two shows—*The Tonight Show Starring Johnny Carson* and *Saturday Night Live*—it was mind-blowing to even consider that one show bore any resemblance to the other. Even then I knew (or I thought I knew) one was real, one was scripted. One was a show where people told true funny stories about their lives, and the other was a show where an actor performed skits wearing a hat that made it look like an arrow was piercing his skull. I didn't know that sometimes what seemed extemporaneous on a talk show had actually been planned beforehand, and that occasionally actors in scripted shows might improvise. That day, with the producer looking expectantly up at me from the notes on her clipboard, I was baffled. Why would I make something up when I had something that was true? What about all the friends and family I'd told the story to who would know I was lying? Plus, in the back of my mind nagged the question: *Was* a Pacer funnier? A Pacer was a car back then that looked like an upside-down bathtub, but it was already a pretty mainstream thing to mock, almost a groan inducer I thought. Wasn't it enough that Jay Leno was nice to an aspiring actress who'd aspired to be here and here she was, perspiring, I mean aspiring?

Around this same time, a few years into the run of *Gilmore Girls,* I had an interview with a journalist for a magazine. I talked about the years I spent studying acting, what it was like to leave New York, my hopes and dreams for the show. At the end, I asked her if she had gotten what she needed and she said she had, but she also seemed a little disappointed.

"I guess—I thought you'd be funnier," she said as she was leaving.

Later, I told my therapist about it. I told her I figured from watching the show that the journalist already knew I *could* be funny, but she didn't know the other things we'd talked about that I thought were equally important. I was trying to add more depth to her understanding.

"It was almost like she didn't really want to know me," I said.

"She probably didn't," my therapist said. "She probably wanted to see the person who made her want to do the interview in the first place."

"But that's a *character,* not a person. It's not the whole picture."

"Well, she writes for a magazine. She's only got room for one or two pages."

But how much of me is that? I wondered. How much of a person fits on two magazine pages?

It seems to me that being a performer is the only job where you are both the car and the billboard advertising it. And what you're willing to reveal is one of the many things for which there is no map or mentor. I came up during a time before anyone used the term "brand" to describe themselves. Especially back then, there was no way to decide how to handle these situations until I was in them. The Honda/Pacer moment was one of the first times I realized there was more illusion to the illusion than I'd ever imagined, that journalists could shape their two pages however they wanted, and only a fraction of any of it was within my control. As early as it was at that point in my career, I could already feel that my instinct when it came to personal information was to pull back. There was nothing I was hiding, nothing in particular that I was afraid of having exposed, it just didn't sit well with me to have my story in someone else's hands. The publicity coming my way at the time was mostly light and positive in nature: a segment on a talk show was one thing, and as I made more appearances on them I grew to understand the need for an occasional fib to guarantee a laugh from the audience before a commercial break. But having something in writing felt more sacred to me. Requests at the time were mostly benign: a magazine article describing "an evening out with," a puff piece about "a day in the life of." Still, although I would not publish my first book until more than a decade later, the seed of the idea that I'd rather tell my own story than have it told by someone else was planted back then. Sometimes a Honda is just a Honda and I'd rather it stay that way. When requests for interviews came in, I began to ask if the format could be "as told to" or if we could just record the conversation and use it verbatim, and those requests ultimately led to what was lurking behind those impulses: I wanted to write it myself instead.

It's funny to me how often people who are not actors ask actors which part of their acting is real and not acting. The job of being an actor is to act as if something is real when it isn't, but people don't always seem satisfied by that explanation. Some of these questions are understandable: "When you played Spider-Man, did you actually have to learn to rappel off a building?" "Was it you or a stunt double in *Mission: Impossible 27B* jumping off that bridge/skyscraper/lava-spewing volcano?" But one that was asked of me, in an on-camera interview by a cocky dude reporter during a press junket for the Diane Keaton/Mandy Moore movie, *Because I*

Said So: "In that scene with all of your butts in underwear, was that really your butt?"

This has never made sense to me. What does it do for you to know if that was my butt or not? (It was.) Does it ruin *Spider-Man* for you if I tell you the webbing is not coming from a hole in his actual wrist? Or if that was all my skating in the pilot of *Mighty Ducks*? (It wasn't.) Don't we all know what's happening here? I feel like we made an agreement when I appeared on-screen and someone called me Blibetta Orkinson. I am not Blibetta Orkinson, but I really want you to believe I am. I spend my days trying to make a pretend story seem as real as I possibly can, and you're left wondering if it was my butt or not?

I don't have the same curiosity. I don't want to see behind the curtain. Illusion is part of what I like in what I see or read. I want to believe that Lady Mary is somewhere having her corset tightened for a banquet for a visiting viscount or whatever. I don't want to hear that they only use the *Downton Abbey* castle for the exteriors, and film the rest at some studio outside of London where the guy playing the wealthy viscount arrives in his convertible Jaguar blasting BTS. I don't want to know!

Over the years I was on *Gilmore Girls,* I can't count how many times I was asked how I knew how to play a mom given that my parents divorced early, and my mom lived overseas for much of my life, and I was mostly raised by my dad. I always struggled to answer this question because there is a real answer, but it might hurt someone's feelings, like those of her mother, my grandmother, who was still very much in my life until she passed away this year at age 101. There is a fake answer that I sometimes gave where I framed having been left by my mother at age four as a positive thing, something that contributed to my being more self-sufficient, an absence that wasn't a loss but was a gift that had made me a stronger person. Because any answer that tried to really answer the question—even the fake one—felt way too vulnerable and for practical journalistic purposes was simply way too long. I learned that most journalists weren't looking for a reply as complicated as: well, yes, it was just me and my dad for a while, and yes my mother mostly lived in London, but I did see her here and there so it isn't like I didn't have a mother at all, and I was very close to her mother, my grandmother, and I had other close family members and even some long-term babysitters who shaped my early years, and my dad remarried and my stepmother played a big part in my later teenage years, and I would say as a generally creative kid who loved to read I've been imagining myself in other people's lives since I wondered what it would be like to be one of the bunnies in *Watership Down* and that part of my brain is probably what led me to become an actor in the first place and I've never once thought of "being a mom" as simply a character trait, there are moms of all kinds, and the fact of being a mom is one part of the given circumstances that I'd consider in order to play any character, but not the only one, and is anyone asking George Clooney if he actually went to medical school to play a doctor on *ER*? Has any actor in any work of Shakespeare murdered someone/ ruled a monarchy/died as the result of a poisonous love pact?

You can understand that this explanation would not fit neatly on the pages of *Entertainment Weekly* or in a tweet from *Vulture*. So, I taught myself another version containing shorter answers that were on a sliding scale of truthful. "I think not growing up with my mom means I didn't have any preconceived notions of what a mom is supposed to be!" I'd chirp. What a reductive spin on a very complex subject! But I was trying to fit myself onto two pages. The truth was that it was painful to talk about her.

Also, it wasn't until I was doing *Gilmore Girls* that DVDs of TV shows started being made and home DVD players became more common. So even though I'd been working off and on for a decade, the first time she saw a significant portion (or really any portion) of what I'd been doing professionally was watching those DVDs. It's possible that during those years she saw me more frequently on TV than in real life, a sort of Honda/Pacer paradox of our own. I was glad she could finally see and appreciate my work, but I'd rather have had the time together in real life.

And no, I've never been a mom, but I have loved a child who lived in my house for a long time who I hope will be a part of the rest of my life and I have loved and felt maternal toward younger friends and my two sisters and my brother, and I love my two nieces and two nephews and the godchild

I have known since he was a week old and I love having Thanksgiving at my house with my family and others I think of as family and I have known great love and devotion and I have given advice but also shut up when I thought I was butting in (with my real butt), and I have worried that any number of people liked what I made for dinner, got home okay, got the job they wanted, were happy in their relationships even if I wasn't totally sure the relationship was best for them, and I have given advice and time and money to these people I love, expecting nothing back, wanting nothing but for them to be happy and healthy and leading a fulfilling life and being a good and kind person. And none of these feelings or actions make me a mom but they are some of what moms feel and do and some moms don't feel or do some of those things but they are still moms.

That night on *The Tonight Show,* I went with the Pacer as a punch line and it fell a little flat. I knew I was lying, and while I supposedly do that professionally, in this case it made me feel self-conscious. I think I would have been a better guest had I just told my story the way it really was. Since then, I've told talk show stories that were completely true and ones that were mostly true but sometimes enhanced a little for comedic purposes, and when being interviewed I have a two-page (or shorter) response on hand, ready to simplify my answers to even the most complex questions.

Is the most important thing to tell the truth, or to tell the truth that will make the audience happy, or to tell another truth entirely, and does it matter if you—the audience—

know which truth I'm telling? Is it better for both of us when I decide which two pages I want you to read? Am I a Honda or a Pacer? I guess I'm a bit of both.

But I'm okay with this contradiction. As long as I'm the one writing my own conclusion.

Old Lady Jackson Takes You to Dinner at 5 P.M.

IN MY FIRST book of essays, I introduced Old Lady Jackson, a kind, slightly conservative grandmother type, a character I'd created during *Parenthood* designed to shield me from seeming uncool or out of touch with my younger co-stars, as in: I love your fifteenth nose piercing, but Old Lady Jackson wonders if maybe you should stop there? And it might sound strange, but since then readers have asked after her, and she's generally sort of taken on a life of her own. So I thought I'd let her take you to dinner at 5 P.M. and tell you how she's been managing her newfound notoriety and what issues have been on her mind lately.

Isn't this a lovely restaurant? I come here most Monday nights for the Early Bird Special. That delicious valet parker Paul keeps my old jalopy right near the entrance for me without my asking; he's going back to community college in the fall, he wants to be a teacher. Now then. It's a bit confusing, but as I understand it there was an author who mentioned me in her book, and her name is Laurel Grimm or something? But also she was on a program called *Glamour Girls*? I tried to watch it once and I was confused by a few things, starting with the title. It's about two friends who seem like lovely young women, but I don't know why you call a show *Glamour Girls* when the wee young lady mainly wears a Catholic school uniform, which is very smart and neat but not exactly remarkable, and the other one wears a strange assortment of hats over pigtails and undershirts with dog faces on them, which I suppose are amusing but can hardly be considered glamorous. And they spoke as if they were being chased by vigilantes. Well anyway, I don't mean to complain, and wasn't it lovely for her to have put me in a book and I'll have to find it in the library next week. I like to go to the library, and anyway I must return my Agatha Christie. But about the television show: I think that mother is my favorite, she says the most wicked things that make me laugh, and isn't the father on it so tall and elegant with a voice like honey? He passed a few years ago someone told me, isn't that sad. Also, they live in the strangest town where they never seem to go anywhere except in circles around and around a sort of open-air shed with flowers growing on it, and there's an attractive man who works at a diner who gives them lots of coffee, and even though he grumbles about it he always seems to give in to Ms. Strange Hats, which honestly seems like a mistake to me, she's had too much coffee already. There's a lovely chef at the local hotel who makes wonderful cakes when she doesn't set them on fire, and a man also works there who seems to be a French businessman, maybe he turns out to be the source of some glamour? Anyway. Maybe I should watch it again. The modern world can be confusing.

I only watch a few things regularly, like *Jeopardy!* But then that sweet Alex Trebek passed, and they couldn't seem to decide who to hire to replace him. That Ken Jennings seems like a respectful boy, and I like that Katie Couric, but how will she have the time to host anything else what with the *Today* show? She does seem very cheery and isn't it important to be cheery in these times that can be so gloomy. I remember LeVar Burton from that space show where he wore a headband over his eyes and I understand he reads to children now too, isn't that lovely?

Oh, here comes the waitress. Can you still call them that? When you've reached my age, it can be hard to keep up. But I do know people like to be called different things now, and it seems to me the least a person can do for another person is to be polite and call them what they'd like to be called. If you told me your name was Barbara and I said I'd rather call you Judy, that wouldn't make any sense, would it? Hello, dear, what's that? Oh yes, I think we are ready to order. Let's see, does the barman make a Sidecar? Wonderful. My Mr. Jackson used to make me one to watch *Jeopardy!* together, and since he's passed I only have them when I go out. I never learned to make them for myself and isn't it a lovely thing to be able to have someone make something for me that reminds me of Mr. Jackson.

I generally try to look on the bright side of life, but there are a few things that vex me. Passwords, for example. I only ever use my password to order an open-faced turkey sandwich from—you've never had one? Oh my, I have them once a week. It's Thanksgiving on a plate. It's white bread, hot but not toasted, with a layer of mashed potatoes and then some turkey sliced not too thick and not too thin and then some gravy on top, very hot. But in order to get my delivery, I not only have to use my password but then have to get a code on my phone and sometimes answer a puzzle that asks how many fire hydrants are in a square and there must be a terrible problem with robots ordering turkey sandwiches because I'm for-ever having to check boxes promising I'm not one, which seems obvious because how many robots do you know who are ordering open-faced turkey sandwiches from the diner? And I'm not sure even a robot could tell the difference what with all the boxes full of fuzzy fire hydrants and blurry palm trees. What a confusion, as Mr. Jackson used to say. Incidentally, my password is MrJackson123! Oh, I don't mind, dear. If a robot wants to order an open-faced turkey sandwich from my account, he's welcome to bring one to his friends in space or wherever they've all been living while at-tempting to sign in to turkey sandwich websites.

I'm also confused by all the thingies you have to have now to watch your shows. I have the Netflax and the Zulu but I'm always forgetting which show is on what and there are so many squares on my screen to choose from. Wouldn't it be easier to put them all in one place? Channels, I believe we used to call them.

Now then, enough of my grizzling. People are always asking me what I've learned over my long life and I'm not sure any of it is of use, but here are a few things. If you're going away for three days, you only need one of everything, but any longer than that you really need two, and it's useful to fill up the car with gas when it's just shy of a quarter of a tank so you never run too low. You should have a gift closet stocked with a few candles and soaps for when you're running over to see a friend whose birthday slipped your mind. Buy wrapping paper in January when it goes on sale and clean out your sock drawer now and then and just throw away ones that are worn, it isn't very dear to buy new ones and it makes you feel grand, a small but a nice boost to have now and then. Sleep in your own spare room if you have one—I did it the other night and a bulb was out in the bedside lamp and the bathroom faucet had a drip, but now it will be nice and ready when my niece comes to visit. My niece is studying some sort of science at the university, and I always tell her you can study science or blueberry waffles as far as I'm concerned; the most important thing is to be a good and kind person. I don't think we remind the children of that enough, and I worry about them all thinking more about their accomplishments or that they need to start companies they sell to Mark Cuban on *Shark Tank* by the time they're 12 years old rather than having a simple, happy life full of friends and books and staring at the sky for no reason. Let's see, what else? You can't believe how easy it is to grow your own herbs just in a little pot somewhere by the kitchen window—a little mint maybe for tea and some basil for salad. A pen at .5 is not too thick and not too thin and oh dear I suppose I have learned a few things well I'll put them all in a Google doc oh don't be surprised. I don't know how to replace my head with a cat while talking to you on the FaceTime or learn that tick tacky dance but I do know how to make a Google doc and pick and choose what else to keep up with just so I can enjoy being in touch with young people such as yourself, which brings me to this.

It's very useful to always have a friend who is much older and one who is much younger. The older friend will remind you what there is to look forward to and the younger friend will keep you telling your stories over again so you'll remember not to forget them. An older friend will tell you you have plenty of time yet, and a younger friend will make you forget time altogether because when you're with them you'll feel, even for a moment, that you're the exact same age.

Now then, let's order. A starter and an entrée and one more Sidecar in honor of Mr. Jackson, wherever he may be, then the sun will just be setting and if you'd like we can make it home in time to watch a *Jeopardy!*

Actor-y Factory

I'M INTERESTED IN how people make things, in the process of how something comes to be. I think most of us are. That would explain the many shows—entire channels even—devoted to watching other people renovate homes we'll never live in, bake foods we'll never eat, and sew garments we'll never wear. I enjoy the process of how nothing turns into something, and it doesn't really matter what that something is. Cooking shows don't make me hungry. House shows don't make me want to move. Those tiny house shows don't make me want to construct a sofa that can also be used as a bathtub. It's just fun to see something change and get better, interesting to witness the choices the creator makes along the way. Sometimes it's even entertaining—or educational—to watch something get worse, like when homeowners decide they want to convert little Jonny's bunk beds into a Jurassic Park theme ride or erect a cabaret stage in the den. "I would never do something *that* crazy!" you might shout at the television while whittling a wooden train from the comfort of the spare bedroom you converted into a year-round Santa's workshop.

Some of what we'll watch is downright bizarre. Like, who decided it would be fun to watch eleven-year-olds compete to make a seven-course meal in under thirty minutes? But we seem to enjoy watching those poor tweens sweating while trying not to cry, which if you think about it is less a cooking show and more a remake of *Lord of the Flies*. What fun? It turns out our appetite for these sorts of shows is endless, so they have to keep inventing new premises. Even though you will never eat the sausage rolls overseen by Paul Hollywood on *The Great British Baking Show,* you have enough curiosity to follow along, or at least I do, presumably because the process, creativity, and intensity of how someone does their job, no matter what that job is, is compelling and relatable.

Many things about being an actor remain mysterious to me. As a kid, I remember watching a TV show and thinking, This person doesn't seem believable to me. That simple recognition and the desire to know more about it was the seed of what eventually became my career. There was a physical feeling I'd get when someone I was watching seemed false, which was different from how I felt when they seemed like they were telling the truth. I have that same response to myself sometimes too—it can be wonky writing I can't make sense of, or something missing in my performance that I can't quite grasp, or a lack of connection with a scene partner. There's a feeling when something is off and a different feeling when the words and energy are carrying you along effortlessly, or are you carrying them? Either way, when emotions and words are flowing, something else takes over. If this doesn't totally make sense to you, you're not alone—it doesn't always make sense to me either. The craft of acting is hard to describe and deeply individual. Some actors can show up to set, say their lines, and afterward go meet a friend for dinner and leave it all behind, while some go through extreme mental and physical duress. I've watched actors cry on cue, and I've watched actors jump up and down until they hyperventilate and hold their face up to a bag of onions to get the same result. But the process of *filming* our sometimes-tortured souls can be quite straightforward, and has a fundamental language, some essential building blocks that are almost always used to tell a story. The making-a-TV-show process is the one I know most about. So, if you've been meaning to go to film school but just haven't found the time, allow me to give you a brief primer on how the acting sausage rolls are made in the Actor-y Factory. (And feel free to use Acting Sausage Rolls as your metal band or drag name.)

As an actor, I'm a worker who is responsible for my piece of a product that will be marketed and sold. In a way, I work in a factory. This is not to equate being an actor to doing actual manual labor in an industrial facility, but a comparison can be made in terms of how parts make up a whole. I don't control the finished product. Once the project I contributed to has been completed, you can choose whether you want to buy it, enjoy it, make fun of it, tell your friends about it, or watch something else. In that way, I'm no different from the pocket on a pair of jeans. "I liked those jeans at first," you might tell a friend. "But after I wore them around for a bit, they stretched out too much." You may have had no issue with the pocket on the jeans, you might even have liked the pocket, but those jeans are still going back to the store. Similarly, you may like a show initially and then get bored when the characters start making choices that are annoying, or maybe you decide it's too taxing to try to get to know new fictional characters altogether when nothing beats *Love Island* (the British one, preferably). So, even though I was only the pocket, if you didn't like the finished product, I'm out of a job. (And also pants-less? I may need to rethink this metaphor.)

Television is probably more of a factory than movies, generally, in terms of which shots and how many are used to tell a story. Network TV is limited by having ads interrupt the story, which dictates that writers end each act with an event of some kind that discourages you from changing the channel. Advertisers want their money's worth, so it tends to be more of a mass-appeal business. If you like your *Chicago Fire* as it is, they're going to serve you what you ordered (hopefully not too burnt. Ahahahblerghsorry). All television has expanded creatively, especially in the last decade, and humbly (because I was briefly on it) I'd submit that a show like *Zoey's Extraordinary Playlist,* where the main character hears other people's thoughts in song, is an example of network TV stretching creatively. But no matter how avantgarde or mass-market, no matter the network or streamer, there exists a basic film language, a shared vocabulary, that everyone uses in order to effectively tell a story.

Let's say you're watching a show that opens with a scene between two people who meet up at a cafe. You might first see a big wide shot: a sunny, busy street, a yellow taxi, autumn leaves falling from a tree. This tells you the basics: what time of year and day it is, what city or town we're in. This establishing shot allows the filmmaker to introduce you to the story and the world of the people in it. It also might give you clues as to the tone—is this a comedy? A drama? Medical dramas rarely open with jaunty music and a sweeping view of the stores on Fifth Avenue all dressed up for Christmas. If you started with a close-up of one of the people in the scene, you'd have no idea whom they were talking to or where they were or what time of year it was or where they got the coffee that miraculously appeared out of nowhere. Short of having a chyron beneath them that read, "We are in a coffee shop in Vancouver in the fall," you'd be lost.

Perhaps, in this opening scene, we see Harry, let's call him, arriving at the coffee shop. Maybe Harry sits down and then looks at his watch or phone, which might tell us he's worried he's late, or maybe he asks a passing waiter for a shot of whisky, which tells us he's nervous. Maybe it's crowded on the patio of the cafe, or it looks like it's going to rain. What if the shot was even wider? What if it began high over all of New York City? This might give us the feeling that Harry's story is a small piece of a much bigger world, and also might indicate that the show had the fancy budget for such a shot. So, lots of big-picture information is there in the master/establishing shot.

Then maybe Glenda, let's call her, arrives and apologizes for being late and orders something from the waiter. She's clutching her bag on her lap in an odd way, and maybe Harry asks if she's okay, and she reaches into her bag, at which point you might need a slightly closer two-shot in which we see both people, or in this case a fifty-fifty in which we see both people in profile, in order to see that Glenda reaches into her bag and hands Harry a live chicken. Since we know where we are from the earlier establishing shot, we don't need to stay in a wide shot looking at all the bustle and crowd of the cafe patio when you'd rather know more about the whole chicken situation. On the other hand, if you were in a tighter single-shot on just Glenda's face in this moment, you wouldn't see the bag she takes the chicken out of and you would be at home screaming WHERE DID THE CHICKEN COME FROM at the television, and your roommate might ask you if you were going insane. But since it's perfectly reasonable (in my brain, for some reason) that Glenda takes a live chicken out of her bag (gently, don't worry), it's important that you at home know she didn't pick the chicken up off the ground or get it from the waiter.

Harry takes the chicken (gently, don't worry), pets him on the head for a moment, and then bursts into tears. At this point, or right before it, you might want to move in to an over-the-shoulder shot, or an "over," which is where you can see a little bit of the back of Glenda, just so you remember she's there and they are sitting together, perhaps followed by a close-up where you're tighter on Harry's face, to see this emotional reaction.

Usually, the decision to use either an over or a close-up is based on whichever one tells the story best, which is obviously a very subjective decision. A close-up can be intense, especially given how many people have one of those 117-inch televisions. But lots of younger people watch TV shows and movies on their computer or phone, which can make these choices more difficult. An over allows you to have a little more breathing room rather than only seeing the actor's face. Some comedy directors believe you use an extreme close-up seldom or not at all. Do I want a close-up on Seth Rogen's face when he slips on the banana peel, or do I want to see him top to toe when he slips on the banana peel? There are mechanics/realities to consider too: perhaps the chicken (whose name is Arthur? Sure) is not a well-behaved chicken, or maybe Arthur is tired (sometimes there's a backup chicken, but not always), and maybe during a few takes while Harry is holding him in the two-shot he starts making crazy chicken noises or pecking Harry's face, and that's a problem not only for the sound department but also for the actor playing Harry, who is trying his best not to be pecked in the face/to cry on cue. So, a closer shot not only allows you to see Harry's reaction but allows the chicken wrangler to take Arthur away for a chicken rest, at which point the props department will hand Glenda a stuffed animal or rubber chicken to hand to Harry so they don't have to mime holding Arthur and instead have something to approximate the live chicken. If you saw the movie *Evan Almighty*—a movie I had a blast doing but that has a 27 percent rating on Rotten Tomatoes (can't win 'em all!), you were looking at many live animals but also some CGI animals, and I was usually looking at neither. I was looking at a very large pile of stuffed animals, and from my stellar (just okay) reactions to this inanimate pile I believe I deserve an adjustment of at least 28 percent from the Tomatometer. Please email your senators on my behalf.

(Speaking of stuffies standing in for real animals, there is nothing more frightening than the rubber babies they give you to hold when the real babies need their chicken rest. On-set pranksters love to pretend they are holding the real baby and then do a pratfall in which they throw the rubber baby high in the air, and I have had approximately seventeen heart attacks over the years as a result.)

Back to Harry and Glenda. In Harry's close-up, the director might tell Glenda she needs to replicate the hand movements she's been doing or mime holding the chicken so that it will match to the wider shots. Or the camera operator might tell her no, they're "clean" of her in this shot, meaning her hands can't be seen and therefore continuity isn't an issue. Or they may say we are "inside," which is a different expression that basically has the same meaning, and also means dozens of times a day on set someone might shout, "We're inside Lauren!" Obviously, we in Hollywood are all adults, except for the chickens and the rubber babies, so when we hear we are "inside" someone, everyone nods solemnly and glances up at the ceiling and tries not to giggle. There's also a shot referred to as the "two-T," which, as you might guess, frames you from your two T's on up. There's a "cowboy shot," which holds you in frame from about midthigh on up, a term coined in old Westerns to ensure you could see the gunslingers' quick draw from their holsters. That one type of shot is named after women's breasts and another after male characters performing acts of violence toward each other is just some good old systemic Hollywood sexism. There's a camera move referred to as the Mickey Rooney, because it's a slow, small creep. Fun!

In the U.S., the area where hair and makeup and the actors' trailers are all parked is called base camp; in Canada it's called circus. In the U.S., the last shot of the day is called the martini, left over from when everyone drank like Don Draper. In Canada it's called the window because you'd get your paycheck at the end of the day, through a . . . window, I guess? I picture it like a bank teller–type setup.

Back to our chicken show. You might wonder why, if Harry has to cry when Glenda hands him the chicken, the director wouldn't start on his close-up so the poor guy doesn't have to cry over and over in the master, where his tears will be farther away and therefore register far less clearly. Firstly, it is very sensitive of you to inquire, and you seem like a lovely person. Sometimes, especially in a particularly emotional scene such as Harry's, you *can* start with the close-up, but there are many more reasons not to. This scene takes place outside during the day, for example, and there are more ways to convincingly light a face to make it look like the sun isn't going down than there are in a wide shot where you'd have to CGI the sky, something this chicken show probably doesn't have the budget for. In the case of chickens and non-rubber babies, they both have restricted hours as mandated by the unions. On *The Mighty Ducks: Game Changers,* the show I'm doing now for Disney+, we are constantly racing against time until the kids "pumpkin," which is the term for when they have to be done with work or we'll all go to jail.

"We can only control what happens between action and cut," is a popular saying among actors. But we don't even really control that. Someone else (the director, the editor, the network or studio) is also going to have an opinion. "Use that one, if you can?" I'll occasionally say to a director after a take I liked, and they will inevitably nod in a vague way that's supposed to be reassuring and then wander off to see about their chicken salad (don't tell Arthur). There are just too many factors to consider in compiling a finished product, and "but that was Lauren's favorite take" is not the most important one. "But that was Brad Pitt's favorite take" might yield a different result, however. I'll have to ask him when he comes over later to play cards. All that talent and a whiz at Gin Rummy too!

But whether you're me or you're Brad Pitt—and if you

happen to be Brad, would you mind picking up some club soda on the way?—one size, one complete take, is rarely used in its entirety anyway for some of the reasons I described in the chicken scene. You'll almost never see an entire scene that stays in the wide shot, or an entire scene that never cuts away from a close-up. An exception might be if a scene is shot as a walk-and-talk, or a "oner," where the camera operator walks (usually) backward with a Steadicam attached to his body. We did a ton of oners using the Steadicam on *Gilmore Girls,* which might be a fun thing to watch for the next time you see it. Oners are lively because the actors are moving and the camera is moving and even though you might not be able to put your finger on it, a shot like this is closer to the energy of seeing something live. But if a loud plane flies overhead or anyone trips or flubs a line, there's nothing else to cut to so you have to go back and start at the beginning. On *Gilmore Girls,* our oners were sometimes so complicated (eleven pages of dialogue during which we circle the gazebo, go up the stairs and through the gazebo, down the stairs, and walk all the way to Luke's) that the camera department would keep a running gate count of how many takes we did before everyone got everything right. I believe the record was somewhere in the high thirties.

In television, the editor will do a first cut for the director, who has starred their favorite takes, and decide where and when to use the close-ups or wide shots. The episodic director does the cut after that, and the showrunner, who in television is usually both the executive producer as well as the head writer, makes the final decisions designed to serve the story (and probably the executives at the network and studio) best. Film is much more of a director's medium, one that seldom consults the writer after they've turned in the script. Another department is going to add popular songs to play under the scenes, or score the piece with original music, and mix the sound in a way that might, say, amplify the chicken clucks to lighten up the scene for comedic effect, and maybe someone else does some CGI to make the chicken behave. This whole process is referred to as "post," short for "post-production." And after all that work is completed, and the piece is "finished," it goes on to marketing, which is another factory unto itself, one that can significantly alter the product we thought we were making. I might have taken the role of Glenda because I thought I was starring in an important show about learning to love, but marketing might decide to put the chicken's face on the poster instead of mine because the chicken tested well with a focus group in Van Nuys. We're making a product, after all, designed to sell and be appealing, and, like the saying goes: Chicken Sells! (It's actually Sex Sells, but Arthur refused to sign the nudity clause.)

If you're an actor or trying to be one, here are a few other random things you should know:

- Someone gets fired from every TV pilot.
- Eleven hundred people weighed in on every decision before you got to work that day, so if the prop person hands you a suitcase you think is ugly, or

not what your character would carry, just be aware
a bunch of people already decided on the one
you're holding, and the prop man probably doesn't
have other options.

- There is a thing in television called a "tone meeting" where, prefilming, every scene is dissected,
and the writer tells the director what the intention
is in each scene, and how he hopes the actors will
play them. So, if you're getting a note from the director that doesn't make sense to you, it may be because she got a note from the showrunner that
doesn't make sense to her either, but it's her job to
try to get it the way the writer envisioned it.

- Most sound departments are excellent at turning
your mic on and off as close to action and cut as
possible. But no one is perfect, and some (very few,
but it's happened) directors even ask them to leave
the mics open so they can hear what actors are saying. Over the years, I've developed a habit of unplugging myself between takes, especially if I'm
complaining about anything/anyone/Arthur the
chicken seeming hungover that day.

- The reason you can't wear your blue shirt is because someone else who is higher up on the call
sheet than you are wanted to wear a blue shirt.

- The reason you can't wear your green shirt is because of the green screen, which will make the part
of you wearing the green shirt invisible.

- Pretty much no one is wearing only their real hair, mostly because hardly anyone's real hair can be made to look good and look the exact same all day, which is important for continuity. And high definition might be great for sports on your TV screen, but it is bad for pores and hairlines. Most hairstylists in the film world use extensions or wigs or sprays to make their actors' hair look hairier.
- Everyone is wrong about which person has the power unless you think the person with the power is Brad Pitt, in which case you might be right. Also, Brad, grab some potato chips?
- Speaking of Brad, during some season of filming *Gilmore Girls* on the Warner Bros. lot, one of the *Ocean's* movies was also shooting. Every day, the cast would play basketball at lunch, and one day I accidentally on purpose walked by them with my extremely beautiful German shepherd (R.I.P., Hannah) and Matt Damon said hi to her. Passing their cars lined up outside the stage where they were filming was the closest I will ever come to attending an exotic car show. The rumor was that the cast never worked longer than eight hours. I give you these details as part of your actor education so that you don't feel bad that it is likely none of this fancy actor lifestyle will ever be true for you or for me.
- A typical filming day for regular people is ten to

twelve hours and I have frequently worked twelve to fourteen hours and a few times on *Gilmore Girls* I worked eighteen to twenty-one hours.

Devastating news: Brad couldn't make it. Could someone else grab the club soda?*

---

* No chickens were harmed in the making of this essay.

Health Camps I Have Hated
(Yet in Most Cases Returned To)

MY FIRST INSIGHT into what being a professional actor might really be like came during the summer of 1988, right after I graduated from college, when I was hired as an Equity apprentice at a regional theater in Michigan. We apprentices sang in the choruses of the musicals and worked in the box office and painted the fences and sewed costumes, all in return for points that contributed toward becoming a member of the theatrical union Actors' Equity. Not only were we unpaid, but we paid a weekly sum to live in a room in the homes of the locals who'd agreed to take us on. The resident ensemble that played the leading roles was comprised of professional actors already in Actors' Equity, brought in mainly from New York City. I'd never known a real working actor, and here I was alongside an entire company of them, many of whom had been on TV or on Broadway, and it was thrilling even to be in the same room with them and hear stories of shows they'd done and auditions they'd been on and generally what their lives were like. They were incredibly generous to us and welcomed our questions with candor. To me, working actors were naturally disciplined people who had figured out whatever the secret was to breaking through to the other side where you might not be rich, but at least you were doing what you loved and not paying fifty dollars a week for the privilege of being in the last row of the chorus of *Oklahoma!* at night and mopping the bathroom floor by day. I quickly learned their lives were more complicated than that.

For one thing, it seemed everyone was making sacrifices of a type I'd never considered. One morning we learned that one of the stars of the Equity company had booked a national tour of a popular Broadway musical. A year of work at least, guaranteed. What a thrill! But later that day I passed her on the pay phone, crying. As she hung up, she turned to me. "It's just that we've had to postpone our honeymoon so many times already," she said, dabbing at her eyes. "But what can I do? I have to take it. It's the lead." One of the older actors told us that in order to be able to drink as much alcohol as he wanted at night, he ate nothing but fruit during the day. "I can get away with it," he said, "because I'm a character man." The two male actors who played most of the main roles were a couple, but outside of our theater pretended they weren't because they worried it ruined something for the mostly female audience. "The price you pay for being a leading man," one of them joked. Another Equity actress arrived fresh from a grueling week at a health spa, and everyone gushed over how well she looked. "I better look good, they fed us nothing but air. What we leading ladies endure, eh?" she said, and booped me lightly on the nose with a well-manicured finger. All this information swirled in a confusing tangle in my mind. I was fascinated by the implied distinctions between, and requirements of, character actor versus lead, never having exactly considered which I might be. All I knew was that I was thrilled to have been booped by the beautiful actress who included me in her category. I concluded that sacrifices and grueling spa experiences must be part of the deal, and I put them on my ever-growing list of what I imagined breaking through to the other side was going to take.

The first time I attempted a week of wellness was at a yoga retreat in upstate New York. It was springtime in the late '90s and I'd just returned to my apartment in Brooklyn after spending my first pilot season in Los Angeles. After being told by every agent and friend and casting person I knew that no one books a pilot the first time they go out for pilot season, I had miraculously booked one—a half-hour sitcom—and was waiting to see if it was going to get picked up. The possibility of being on a series that might air on television was brand-new. The possibility of having *any* sort of steady job and not living paycheck to paycheck was even more novel, something I could hardly imagine. I'd just spent three months sleeping on my aunt's couch and driving in from Long Beach to Los Angeles for auditions every day, an hour each way on the 710 freeway. If I had a long break in between appointments, I'd camp out at the food court in the giant, centrally located mall the Beverly Center. I had a few thousand dollars in the bank from some commercials I'd done, but I'd left my job as an SAT tutor and turned in my apron at the Mexican restaurant where I'd been waitressing in Park Slope, Brooklyn. I'd gambled and didn't yet know if I'd won. I'd just made some money on the pilot, but the paycheck from a single episode of television would not last long if I went back to being an unemployed actor in New York City. So maybe part of the appeal of entering a rigorous, structured environment was that it offered me a sense of relief from what had been a risky, unpredictable time.

The yoga retreat was in the woods somewhere and it was always cold and there was no TV and zero cell phone reception, perhaps largely because most people didn't yet have cell phones. There was, however, a single phone booth in the communal lounge—an actual booth with a narrow bench you could sit on and a folding glass door you could close for privacy, similar to the ones that used to be on every corner in Manhattan—and at night guests would line up to make their calls. The time limit was a strict fifteen minutes, and one night I was on the phone with my agent, still a thrilling novelty, and while I thought I had my eye on the clock, I was startled when a woman banged on the glass with the palms of her hands and yelled: "It's *my* turn! It's *my* turn now!" Hunger plus isolation plus a constant chill in the air can make a lady cranky.

My pilot did not get picked up, but I had enough encouragement from my agents and a few casting people who were bringing me in to audition regularly (thank you, Marc Hirschfeld), that I decided to make the move to Los Angeles anyway, and I continued to march bravely up the wellness mountain, choosing the next spa because I'd heard Oprah had gone there. Before there was social media showing us makeup tutorials and perfect sourdough loaves and making us feel like everybody else was having more fun, we had glossy magazines that basically did the same thing, and when I read an article about the "transformative" experience Oprah had at this retreat, I was thrilled to be able to try it myself. The resort was in the mountains north of Los Angeles in a modest structure that felt like a well-worn family home. The rooms were small, and the walls were so thin you could hear the squeak of the mattress in the next room if your neighbor turned over in the night. Once again there was no TV. The place was popular because of the physical and spiritual results that it supposedly produced, and the number of rooms was so limited that there was a months-long waiting list, and sometimes, due to overflow, they'd house people in what was basically a screened-in porch. In addition to hearing Oprah had gone there, I'd also heard that one day she was so hungry she asked to have an additional hard-boiled egg at breakfast. The meal plan was very strict, no exceptions given, and

Oprah was told she couldn't have another egg. Oprah insisted she be given an additional egg, and while they eventually caved in and gave her the egg, as a punishment they took an egg away from everyone else. I have no idea if this is true or just Hollywood lore, like the rumor circulating back then that one of the ways Jennifer Aniston stayed so thin was by smoking a rare medicinal strain of marijuana that didn't give you the munchies.

Among my fellow spa-goers were a rowdy group of men who all worked for the same bank and had flown in on a private plane from Las Vegas the night before after literally ordering everything on the left side of the menu at Nobu because they could. They all felt ill on our first day and several of them threw up on our hike. None of them had seen anything I'd been in, but when someone told them I was an actress they proceeded to call me "Hollywood" for the rest of the trip, and frankly, I sort of loved it. At night, to try to keep us entertained and distracted from the lack of television, the Oprah spa brought in various speakers, one of whom was a handwriting analyst who told me based on my writing sample that I was very detail-oriented and could have a great career in finance.

A girl I'd met because she worked out at the same gym at the same time I did told me she'd spent every weekend for a month at a retreat in the desert a few hours away from Los Angeles. "I feel amazing," she told me. "It's the answer." Without bothering to ask what the question was, I booked myself into the next available slot. The entrance to the retreat was down a dusty, unmarked road that passed by a trailer park enclosed by a twisted barbed wire fence. The place had a sort of groovy '70s vibe, by which I mean their tiny pool didn't seem clean enough to swim in, and—you guessed it— no TV. During the day, meals consisted only of juices in which you mixed a smelly green powder that you scooped out from a giant glass jar. At night, hot soup was served from a single urn in the common area, and all the ladies would line up to wait their turn with an air of thinly veiled desperation not unlike the vibe of the upstate New York phone booth line.

While other spa-type treatments were available, the focus of this retreat was on the health benefits of receiving daily colonics. I'd like to take this opportunity to thank every co-lonicist (?) I've ever had. This cannot be an easy job. Yet most of the women I've met on the other end of the tube (sorry) are the sweetest and happiest people I've ever encountered. They seem satisfied when their work produces visible results (sorry) and comment happily on what they're seeing as if running into old classmates at a high school reunion: "Oh look, it's Carol! Haven't seen her in a while. And . . . I think I see Kyle over there—yep, that's Kyle all right—wow, he started slow, but he sure is speeding up now! Ooh, great, here comes Rob, he can be *very* hard to reach."

My only beef (sorry?) is that I've sometimes noticed a tendency toward an attempt at upsell from these kind ladies, as if I'm ordering from a waiter pushing specials during happy hour at a TGI Fridays rather than undergoing a clinical procedure designed to vacuum out my guts. Did you know that you don't have to be resigned to having just plain old water in your colonic, no sir! If you want to treat yourself, you can upgrade with add-ons like liquid vitamin B for energy, collagen for protein, or if you just need a quick pick-me-up, a shot of coffee might be your thing! And you thought there was only one way to get that caffeine fix.

You may think these places are teeming with Hollywood folk trying to shed the two pounds they don't need to lose, and I have always heard they are, but I've hardly ever seen another actor on any of these trips. Although on one of them a woman who worked in the spa told me there was a suite they'd affectionately dubbed "the Matthew McConaughey room" because he had an extended stay there while preparing to play the emaciated AIDS patient in *Dallas Buyers Club*. I have no idea if this is true, but the woman said he was very charming throughout his starvation.

Maybe it was because almost none of these places were as great as their hype that I kept trying to find one that was? One year, I asked my sister Shade to come with me to a boot camp in the Santa Monica Mountains that I'd heard was great. She knew my stories of camps of the past and was understandably wary. I convinced her by assuring her this trip would be different: it was only a long weekend, not a whole week, and the accommodations were in a five-star hotel where we'd have access to all its amenities. "Can we leave if we hate it?" she asked. I assured her we could.

It turned out there would be no time to enjoy any amenities, five-star or otherwise, because we were all to report in the lobby each day at 5 A.M. Rather than having the trip leaders call our rooms individually, we were each given a walkie-talkie and instructed to leave it on all night so that when it screeched to life at 4:30 A.M. with the loud, cheery voice of one of the guides, we'd be sure to wake up. This was one of the scariest ways to be woken up I've ever experienced, and I turned my walkie-talkie off after the first day. The health plan here consisted mainly of hiking for hours and hours, and on the first day we realized the early wake-up time was because by 11 A.M. the sun became cartoonishly blazing hot. On our second day of cartoon heat, one of the campers muttered something about wondering why we were all paying to hike in mountains whose trails were free of charge, and we all stopped and looked at each other in miserable revelation. Later that day, a couple left for "medical reasons," but could barely contain their giggling as they departed, and my sister and I felt our window for doing the same had somehow closed. This camp tried to make the evenings fun by offering various lectures just like the No Egg for Oprah place had, and one night they brought in a psychic who gushed over my sister, telling her she was destined to run a company one day, but during my reading struggled to see anything hopeful or positive. "Are you in finance?" she asked me. No. No, I am not. Plus, the aspect of being in a hotel, which had once seemed a promising element, turned out to be depressing. We'd return from our day on the trail overheated and caked with dirt and straggle dejectedly past well-dressed diners and clean-haired partygoers clinking glasses and cutting into steaks. My sister has pledged that from now on we only go to nice hotels to do nice hotel things.

Finally, I decided I was ready to graduate from these bare-bones boot camps to a place whose focus was gentler and more luxurious. I booked a trip to an expensive retreat I'd read about near San Diego, and I wondered if my trusty friend Kathy would want to join. But Kathy had just had a baby (my godson, Clyde) and I worried she wouldn't want to tear herself away from—"I'm in," she said, almost before the invitation left my mouth. Kathy and I have been friends since we were eighteen years old, and we felt very mature choosing to celebrate health in our 40s rather than wasting our precious vacation time drinking margaritas on some silly, relaxing beach in Cancún. In the car on the way we chatted and reminisced about our time together as undergrads and the fun we had being roommates back in Brooklyn. Kathy had never been to one of these retreats, and in describing to her what I thought it was going to be like based on my past experiences, we both began to panic a little, so we pulled over and stopped at a Burger King and ordered an amount of food neither of us would ever have considered on a normal day. When we arrived at the spa, a man was waiting at the entrance to help with our bags, and as we opened the car doors a bunch of burger wrappers spilled out on the ground at his feet. He pretended not to notice.

The rooms at this camp were far more upscale than the ones at the others I'd visited, although still no TV. It's not that I'm a TV addict, but while staying in a strange place and undergoing a day of exertion, my brain doesn't want to be alone with its thoughts, it wants an episode of *The Voice*. The rumor here was that as nice as the rooms might seem to normal people, Barbra Streisand had hers recarpeted before her stay. I also have no idea if this is true, and come to think of it, this rumor may have been about Martha Stewart, I forget.

You could choose which activities you wanted and have as vigorous or relaxing a day as you pleased—no walkie-talkies blaring at 5 A.M. here. They also offered facials and massages and other services that made it feel less prison-y, which was nice. There was a gift shop with a selection of candles and caftans, and boy do your fashion tastes change when you're very hungry and limited to a small selection of candles and caftans. Kathy revealed that she'd smuggled in a box of Weight Watchers 100-calorie wafers, and throughout our stay a highlight was cutting one of the wafers in half and sharing our measly portions, savoring them along with our evening cups of weak herbal tea. Other attendees that week included a famous ice skater and a writer I admired, and we were told every First Lady in history had also been a guest, which made us feel fancy. There was a semi-spiritual ceremony on the last night in which we all gathered in a circle around a bonfire and were asked to figuratively "throw something away" that was "holding us back," which made me wonder if they somehow knew about the empty Weight Watchers wafer wrappers in my pocket.

Why, you may wonder, do I go to these Hell camps, I

mean Health camps? What—if anything—do I get out of this repeated semi-torture? Well, I do like a challenge and a feeling of accomplishment. Especially when I was in my 20s and 30s, I noticed a direct correlation between how thin I was and how much work I got. And while I've long since learned that a week of even the most strenuous activity and clean eating cannot make a lasting difference, I enjoy the concept and the feeling of a reset. Think of all the electronic glitches that can be fixed simply by unplugging and restarting—what if it worked like that for people too? It's like putting money in the bank that can later be used for a bagel and cream cheese withdrawal. Some of these trips were before an event or while I was on a book deadline, and being away from my usual routine gave me a helpful boost. And while some people probably sit down to dinner and think to themselves: Is this meal good for my health? I've spent years at every dinner asking myself: Is this meal good for my career? and that becomes tedious and tiring, and going somewhere where everything is preplanned and there are zero choices to make is a relief. As messed up as it may be, I know very few actresses who aren't in constant pursuit of losing five pounds, and I guess the illusion of these places is you can pay to have someone else do it for you. Ironically, all this effort has been in pursuit of what perhaps is an illusion of achieving a state of effortlessness, of one day becoming one of those people who aren't constantly stressing over the balance of how to be healthy but also enjoy life. Have I really learned anything at any of these supposedly transformative places? I'm not sure. The founder of one of the camps told us the most valuable advice she could give was to work out first thing in the morning to get it out of the way. That I've spent zillions of dollars only to walk away with that simple wisdom may not seem worth it, but it stuck with me, and I pass it on to you. Oh, and I guess I've also learned that if acting doesn't work out, my brilliant career in finance awaits.

If you are eyeing one of these "vacations," I hope you've enjoyed this, the one and only Yelp review I've ever given. As a result, I may be barred from ever attending another spa in the United States again, but I've been googling one in Austria I'm curious about. I don't know if this is true, but the rumor is Beyoncé goes for two weeks every year, the rooms overlook a beautiful lake, and most importantly, they have television.

Forever 32

The first time I ever wondered what it might be like to some-day be 32 years old was when I was 22 years old and in acting school preparing for a part in the John Patrick Shanley play *Savage in Limbo*. At the time, the attempt to unlock the mystery of how to play someone a decade older than me felt as daunting a challenge as I imagined the effort of taking on one of the great Shakespearean classics would be or preparing myself for the type of role that might put Daniel Day-Lewis in the running for another Oscar. Did I need to, at least in part, tackle this immense transformation physically, I wondered, as we'd been taught in our movement classes when playing characters very different from ourselves? Would a thirty-two-year-old woman walk with stooped shoulders perhaps, or maybe a limp, as a result of her decrepit agedness?

These were actual considerations I gave at the time, possibly because the language of these Shanley characters that I found so inspiring and touching was so specifically New York—poetic and gruff and fundamentally the language of the deeply depressed—that I thusly concluded that being older must be accompanied by innate sadness and brokenness. My character, Linda Rotunda, says things about herself like, "I'm so ashamed. I feel ugly. I feel fat," for example. All the characters in the play are 32 years old as stated in the stage directions, and none of them were particularly happy or successful. The conclusion I drew from this very limited field research of one single play and one single character who seemed obsessed by life passing her by at the inconceivably elderly age of 32 was that arriving there was not going to be a party.

And then I arrived there. When I turned 32, I'd been living in Los Angeles for almost three years. I was as healthy and happy as I'd ever been. I had good friends, fun weekly game nights, a sweet boyfriend, and frequent sushi dinners out. I was 32 years old, but I wasn't depressed or world-weary. In fact, I was living a reality that had once only been a dream: I was supporting myself financially as an actor without the assistance of a day job for the first time, ever. Over these three years I'd somehow managed to compile a yearly—if unpredictable—mix of jobs in independent films, recurring TV guest spots, parts on short-lived series that got canceled in their first season, and pilots that didn't get picked up. This assortment had not created job security exactly, but it had proved consistent enough over time to have allowed me to acquire my first new car (a Ford Explorer Sport two-door—I don't think they make them anymore—black with tan leather interior, which was all the rage then), a cute duplex bungalow rental from the '20s with hardwood floors and an outdoor patio, the first savings account that wasn't chronically hovering near zero, and a growing list of "my people." I had never had people before. By "people" I mean resources—experts and specialists, helpers in areas in which I was inexpert. People who were inessential in that they weren't going to save my teeth from rotting or check my cholesterol, but who suddenly seemed necessary here in my mildly successful life as an actor. I suddenly had multiple hair people, for example. I don't remember having a single hair person at all in New York. I don't remember ever getting my hair cut there. I hennaed it myself once, which turned it eggplant purple, and I don't even remember doing anything about it. I just let it fade, I guess?

But beyond my less–purple–in–Los Angeles hair, at 32 I also started to realize I had a sense of myself I'd never had before. I had ambition and hopes to keep going beyond what I'd already achieved, but I also had a sense of satisfaction I didn't remember having in my 20s. I wasn't worried about getting older and I didn't wish I were any younger. I felt I was the age I was, which was a novel sensation. It was that year that I was cast in *Gilmore Girls*. I didn't know it yet, but it was the beginning of something that would define me.

Mae Whitman and I connected from the moment we met on the set of *Parenthood,* when I was in my 40s and she was only 19. She seemed so much younger than me then, but over the years our friendship became less mother-daughter and more one of equals. By the time she was in her early 30s and I was in my early 50s, we found we liked doing many of the same things with many of the same people, and that our age gap only came up once in a while, like when we talked about shopping one day and she mentioned a cool clothing store in Echo Park and I mentioned stopping in to Neiman Marcus and we turned to each other and said, in unison, "What's that?" Mae had to tell me aviator sunglasses were "over," and I begged her to stop drowning herself in the baggy tie-dye sweatshirts she collected from vintage stores. We had some typical generational disputes.

But we kept discovering we had more things in common than we had differences. Mae and I have both been in show business for about the same amount of time, for example. Her first professional job was about twenty-five years ago in a commercial for Tyson's chicken, and mine was about twenty-five years ago in an ad for Walmart sweaters where my first on-camera line was the very dramatic and complex: "What the heck, get a turtleneck." Because Mae is fundamentally an old soul and was exposed to so many adults on all the sets she grew up on, we shared a lot of music and movie references, although I was proud to weep along with her when I showed her *Terms of Endearment,* one of my favorite movies she somehow hadn't yet seen. And her ambition and enthusiasm regarding her career and her relationships and shoring up her self-esteem, and her basic joyful view of life, inspired me and reminded me a little of myself at that age.

Just for fun, we began to take note of these recurring connections that sprung from our different perspectives/ ages, and for some reason, we started referring to them as our "podcast." Once, I told Mae that *Shark Tank* was a really enjoyable show and she sort of rolled her eyes at me but she watched it anyway and eventually she became totally hooked on it and met and became friends with Lori Greiner, one of the main *Shark Tank* hosts, and I, faux-outraged, demanded we discuss this on our podcast, which led to the idea for "Ask Lori," a reoccurring imaginary financial advice segment on our weekly imaginary podcast.

We began to discuss other possibilities for this nonexistent show. We could do a rewatch of the series where we met, *Parenthood,* and invite former cast members to guest on our podcast. Mae suggested we open each podcast episode with a guided meditation in which we pretended to be sipping margaritas in Mexico or sitting in a cafe in Paris. We'd share the recipes for the drinks we were supposedly drinking and maybe give travel advice for the location where we were pretending to drink them. Each week, we'd choose an impressive but obscure historically relevant female and talk about her accomplishments in a segment we'd call "Woman of the Week." We imagined our actor friends as guests, but wanted to feature non-actor friends as well, and learn more about their careers: clothing designer Rachel Antonoff, author friends like Jennifer E. Smith and Jenny Han, producer Jessica Vitkus.

We'd have a book club and a song of the week, and test products and review the ones we liked for a segment called "Will You Be Our Sponsor?" We'd rummage through our closets for outdated or unused items for a segment called "Why Do I Even Still Own This?" For a time, every laugh we shared became a potential podcast feature. One day, Mae commented on something being the "saddest sentence she'd ever heard" and we even wondered if that could be a sort of competition segment between us.

This was all happening during peak pandemic 2021, where we'd spend many days sitting outside on my porch and wondering aloud about when or if filming would start again and when or if we'd ever return to either of our series, both of which were in limbo during this time. I think dreaming up the podcast was one way of not only having an outlet for our frustrated creative selves, but also just having fun imagining a more hopeful future during a bleak time.

And then we sold the podcast! We decided to call it *50/30,* a nod to the 20-year gap in our ages. We were excited to have the backing of a successful company and the creative input from an experienced producer. Yet almost immediately, thinking about and working on the podcast became . . . a lot less fun. What had flowed organically now felt stuck somehow, and the dozens of ideas it seemed we'd been having daily pretty much dried up. In my little graduation speech book, *In Conclusion, Don't Worry About It,* I mention some early advice that always stuck with me when I was first starting out: do every job as if you're being well paid. That advice helped remind me to take pride in my work whether I was waitressing or painting fences at summer stock or holding a tray as a cater waiter at the hundredth wedding. But this was something I hadn't encountered before: do a job as if it's something you're still only doing for fun even though now there are deadlines and expectations and money attached. It occurred to me that there was a reason most other podcasts were structured by rewatching or recapping TV shows or movies or hosting weekly guests. Like any talk show, the personality of the host is important, but it's a lot of pressure to rest a whole show on two people chatting and segments about whose sentence is sadder. The few episodes we recorded were enjoyable but also felt too unstructured. We both started to feel self-conscious when either of us said something funny or whenever we had one of our multigenerational misunderstandings. Should we stop what we were doing and press record?? This friendship/commerce overlap didn't bother Mae as much—she has a natural candor and ease with everyone, and I think she'd be an excellent host on her own. But we both felt to some degree that trying to entertain people with our friendship was putting a strain on our friendship. After much discussion, we bowed out of *50/30.*

I am lucky to have friends of all ages: the cast of *Mighty*

Ducks are mostly teenagers; my godson and his crew are in their early twenties; my sisters and brother aren't yet 40; Jen Smith and the writer friends I've made are mostly in their 40s; my peers and I are in our 50s; my dad, my dear friend and Gilmore mom Kelly Bishop, and my friend and literary agent Esther Newberg are in their 60s and beyond. My cast always tells me they feel older than they are, feel older than how people treat them. My friends in their 20s feel like they are racing against some sort of clock of success, my friends in their 30s are full of their careers and figuring out relationships, and most of the older people I know are surprised to find they aren't in their 30s anymore. My grandmother used to say the only way she knew she wasn't 18 anymore was when she looked in the mirror, and that makes more sense to me now.

I'm a de facto grandma to my 2-year-old niece, Kit, and I've been spending lots of time with her lately. Considering how far away I thought my 30s were when I was in my 20s, Kit and I have more in common than I'd expect. We both like to holdy-hands when crossing the street, and we both love to spend a vacation day going swimmy-swimmy. Neither of us likes naps or olives, and while our musical tastes differ slightly, I do understand what's catchy about that "Baby Shark" song. I see the beauty in her lumpy bedtime companion whom the rest of the family call Ugly Bear, and we both love poring over the dog-eared pages of my childhood books of nursery rhymes, although my sister had to inform me that the poem about Wee Willie Winkie—a character who runs around town in his nightgown looking into children's bedroom windows to see if they've fallen asleep yet—was now considered creepy. I feel I'm at an age now, like I was at 32, where I'm not doing too much looking forward, and not getting too stuck on looking back, but feeling that no matter their age or mine, I'm happy that I have these friends, and these precious days to spend with them.

Squirrel Signs

I'VE SAID IT before but I'm happy for any opportunity to say it again: getting to do *Gilmore Girls: A Year in the Life* for Netflix was one of the best, happiest, most rewarding experiences of my career. I know not all of you got the final four words you hoped for, but returning to that idyllic town and those quirky characters and Amy and Dan's dense and bubbly language almost literally lifted me off the ground some days. At the end of filming there was the inevitable slump, a post-Christmas feeling when something you've spent so much time looking forward to has happily exceeded expectations but has sadly come to an end. But I was reenergized too, having been reminded how much I loved being an actor, and I was excited to bring that renewed spirit to whatever was to come next.

Most actors I know—even successful, professional ones—immediately finish a job and wake up the next morning with complete certainty that they will never work again. This is not like when you're impressed by how well you blow-dried your hair one morning but you're trying not to gloat about it so you turn to your co-worker and shrug your shoulders and say, "Gah, my hair is just impossible today," in order to get them to tell you you're totally wrong and in fact your hair has never looked better. The "I'll never work again" is more serious because if you're an actor, no matter how many other successful actors you know, it is not just paranoia, it has happened to someone close to you. Someone who once told you they'd never work again, sometimes . . . doesn't. It might have been their choice, but sometimes not, and this mystery of why it happens and to whom and when hangs heavily somewhere in the back of every actor's psyche. These are not careers that are guaranteed to age along with us, and maybe what worked in our 20s just doesn't translate into every other decade, but there's no way of knowing that until the day when the business lets us know it doesn't need us anymore. But for once, just for a tiny moment, after this incredible experience, I allowed myself to think, softly, in the back of my mind, "Hey, I think I might actually work again."

One funny thing about having a longish career is that once you've gotten to a certain place, choices can become more difficult to make. If you've played a lovable veterinarian on a successful show for many years, for example, you may think it wouldn't be a great idea to play another lovable veterinarian, but the offers or auditions coming in are mostly from people who just want to see you do what they already know you can do, which is play a lovable veterinarian. My career path had been unusual in that it was as logical as if I had some sort of corporate job where a small role led to a slightly bigger one, which, with hard work and persistence, eventually led to a corner office. I'd had downs and I'd had ups, but they'd progressed from one to the other logically and at least somewhat predictably. So, while I knew I might have to wade through some lovable veterinarian offers, I figured it wouldn't be long before something else came my way. In the meantime, I'd begun pursuing work as a screenwriter. I'd only had one assignment so far—adapting my novel *Someday, Someday, Maybe* as a TV pilot through Ellen DeGeneres's production company—but I went in search of more.

I found a book that I thought could be a movie, and to my surprise no one had optioned it, so I reached out to the writers and I optioned the book, and got a meeting with an executive who said she had read my novel and loved it, and had read the book I'd optioned and loved that too, and she thought I was the perfect person to adapt it, and I sold it in the room. I was very excited, especially because "sold it in the room" means exactly what it sounds like—a person who has the clout to do so says yes, and you're hired. This rarely happens. Studios are companies like any other where teams of people make decisions, except it's ten times more stressful because executives are endlessly being replaced by new executives with "fresh voices," who will ultimately also be thrown out in search of fresher, newer voices, and everyone runs around panicked they're about to lose their job because often, they are. Usually, the person you're meeting with is not the person in the position to give the go-ahead and they need to check with someone or many someones, so that if the movie is a success the person who greenlit it doesn't become too power-hungry and start asking for raises and if the movie turns out to be a dud there's shared blame and they stand a chance of staying fresh and new for a little while longer. Once you've sold something in the room, you realize that was always a possibility, and it is likely that anyone who told you "It wasn't my decision to make" or that they had to "run it up the chain of command" in the past was actually the equivalent of a used car salesman telling you that while he'd love to give you a lower price on the used Toyota you have your eyes on, first he has to check with the boss. They . . . were lying. There's a jewelry store in Beverly Hills that I love for its confusing combination of feeling very fancy while simultaneously feeling like a mysterious holdover from the jewelry district in Manhattan. Every time I've been there, if the salesperson gets the idea I might be remotely interested in something, she'll look both ways and lower her voice to a whisper. "You want me to see if I can get you a lower price, miss? Let me see what my manager can do for you." Then she disappears in the back, probably counts to twenty or calls her grandson, and comes back to me with a better price. And I'm thrilled every time.

My adaptation stayed as true to the book as I could manage. Why wouldn't it? We'd both agreed we loved the book and that it would make a great movie. There was never any discussion of changing it in any significant way. I worked on it for three months straight, and turned it in, and a meeting was scheduled for me to hear what the head executive and her team thought of it. In addition to the executive I'd had the original meeting with, there were three other people in the room whom I'd never met. When I entered, everyone was typing into their phones but looked up and smiled: "Isn't the traffic terrible? Are you loving this weather?! Where'd you get your shoes? Why'd they cancel *Parenthood*?" Then they all went back to their phones.

Unsure as to which answers to give to whom and in what order, I smiled and said, "Great to see you all!" which seemed satisfactory in that there were no follow-up questions. Then there was sort of an awkward beat where the three new people went back and forth between looking at their boss and their phones. I felt like I was in an improv class whose rules I didn't understand.

"What did you think of the script?" I asked them, and they all turned to me, startled. Since then, I've learned it's almost never a good idea when pitching, auditioning, making dinner for someone, or going on a date to ask what someone thinks of the thing you wrote/scene you just performed/dish you cooked/face you showed up to the date with. If they like something about it/you, they'll volunteer that information.

Finally, "Fun characters," one executive said.

"Oh, thanks!" I said.

"I liked the . . . lines they say?" another said, squinting at her cell phone.

"Oh, the, the dialogue?" I asked, and she nodded into her phone.

"I love Boston," another said, mercifully not on his phone but rather vaguely gazing at a point somewhere over the top of my head, lost for a moment in what I assumed were his fond memories of traveling to Boston. I like Boston too, and it would be a great backdrop for any movie, but my script did not take place in Boston. "Me too!" I said, because over the years I have come to at least somewhat understand the rules of show business.

Over the course of the meeting about the script, it became clear to me that maybe, *maybe* one of the people in the room had read it, but even that person may have just read someone else's summary of it, and no one seemed to have any specific notes or comments, and they all frankly seemed to be winging it. Have you ever been stuck at a table at a wedding with people you've been told you've met before, and had to improvise your way through not knowing/not remembering them? "Sally, how've you been since the . . . party . . . I mean restaurant . . . that place where we met?" It was like that.

"You know what I'm realizing?" the head executive said. All eyes turned to her in reverence. FINALLY! This was going to be the breakthrough we all wanted. Everyone put their phone down and sat up a little straighter. I sighed in relief. I suddenly understood why the meeting had felt so off. The other executives had held back in order to let their boss take the lead. Duh. It's almost as if I forgot all the rules of show business for a minute! Waiting for her to give her opinion first was the explanation for all the phone scrolling, vague looks, Boston.

"I don't think there's a movie in this book," she said.

"I'm—sorry, what?" I said.

"I just don't find it cinematic enough. It's as if this book is more of a book than it is a movie."

After a moment where everyone seemed frozen, they all began nodding their heads and murmuring their agreement. I wasn't sure what to do or say. The script felt like a book because it had been a book, which was at one time its strength, but that trait had now become its weakness, never mind my lingering confusion over how Boston was involved. The executive continued, saying that she'd actually never really liked the book or considered its subject matter relevant, and that she was just realizing now that the thing she'd most liked about it was the title and would I be interested in coming up with an entirely different plot that had nothing at all to do with the book except for copying its title?

"Just the . . . title?"

Even in the shock of the moment I knew I could not go to the writers whose book I'd optioned and ask if I could throw all their work out. So I passed. This confusing encounter was just the beginning of a year—or was it two—where it seemed I did *not* understand the rules of show business and every road I went down was blocked in some way, and nary a lovable or nonlovable veterinarian came my way. Occasionally something would come my way that wished it were *Gilmore Girls,* and occasionally—and confusingly—a script would come my way that wished it were *Breaking Bad.* I watched every episode of *Breaking Bad* and yes, I was trying to get away from lovable vet, but none of these scripts came close to the original and they all involved me committing murders and endlessly being covered in either blood or mud or both, and just . . . no. Like any out-of-work actor, I turned to playing a compulsive amount of Scrabble on my phone. Phone Scrabble does not penalize you for trying words that are not words. Occasionally I'd input a bunch of letters and come up with a winner. But usually not. Did you know that "bleepjep" is not a word? I do!

Finally, some relief came in the form of an offer on a half-hour script I loved with an actor I loved already attached and a well-respected producer also attached. The word was that this script was the producer's passion project and that any number of networks and streamers were interested in working with him, and there would probably be a very competitive market for the project. The deal-making process was easy, the meetings were set, enthusiasm was high, and . . . the producer died. This was unexpected and shocking and sad, and the least important part of this loss was that the enthusiasm for the project waned perhaps partially as a result, but there it was, another block in what had looked to finally be an open road.

In the meantime, one birthday had passed—or was it two—and another one approached. Do you know that "hop-bib" is not a word? I do! As my birthday drew closer, I asked anyone who might be listening to send me a sign. Send me a sign telling me what else I can do, I whispered. Send me a sign that things are looking up.

In my house there are French doors off the dining room that lead to a little porch. In the summer I like to leave the doors wide open all day, and I'd done this for years without incident. On my birthday I cracked them only slightly and turned to grab something from the kitchen and when I came back to open them all the way there was a squirrel sitting in the middle of my dining room table staring at me. I probably screamed, which caused the squirrel to jump onto the curtains that flank the French doors, thereby blocking my ability to open the doors further without having to come closer to the intruder than I dared. I hovered in the doorway between the kitchen and the dining room, and the squirrel hung on to the curtain and we both stayed like that for what could have been fifteen minutes. What if the squirrel panicked and jumped down from the curtains and ran upstairs and got into the bedrooms or a closet and hid there? How would I ever get him out? I did nothing but wonder what the future held for me and my squirrel for the next hour. He didn't move from the curtain.

Thankfully, a friend who'd grown up on a farm stopped by to wish me a happy birthday and he rolled his eyes at my city-girl fears and picked the squirrel off of the curtain with his bare hands and set him free outside.

Later, after my heart stopped pounding, the realization dawned. A squirrel had come to visit me in my house on my birthday. Talk about a sign! Except . . . there was nothing I could find about the symbolism of squirrels, no culture that seemed to view them as significant, no squirrel history I could derive any meaning from, fortuitous or otherwise. Maybe the squirrel was a sign that I needed to stop looking for signs and draw my own conclusions? Maybe I needed to gather my nuts? Be more resourceful? Eat more avocados?

The phone remained silent.

I tried to stay positive. I took a few smaller voice-over jobs I may not have normally been interested in. I didn't listen to the voices telling me my time might be up. Or rather, I tried to limit the amount of space they were allowed in my day. What good would it do me to indulge them? Mine is a business, like so many, where things happen mostly beyond my control. The best defense, I've learned, is to be conscious of the only thing I *can* control: what it is I'm doing in the space between my ears. I tried to keep my thoughts humble and upbeat. It wasn't always easy. And nothing I did during this time was what caused the phone to ring, which it eventually did. But everything I practiced helped me stay a little bit saner while I waited for a break in the clouds. Except maybe my obsession with Scrabble, which morphed from helpful distraction to cause for concern. No one cares that "tamquit" is not a word, Lauren! I decided to give it a rest for a while.

A few years ago, I rented a beach house for a week in the summer and I came home one day to find I'd been robbed: lamps were turned over, papers thrown to the ground. Except it turned out it wasn't a burglar; it was a squirrel that'd come in through the chimney and gotten stuck in the house. I finally got him out with the help of some lovely animal control people, and I wondered: Is *this* squirrel a sign? Why else do squirrels keep breaking into my houses? Recently, I worked with a trained squirrel actor on set. Was *this* squirrel a sign? I mean, how many people do you know who've had one significant squirrel encounter, let alone three? Surely there's a sign somewhere in there?

The trained squirrel's name was Brooklyn. I used to live in Brooklyn. I'm destined to move back to Brooklyn? Or maybe not. I guess sometimes a squirrel is just a squirrel, but I'm still going to keep looking on the bright side.

Red Hat, Blue Hat

IN PREPARATION TO direct for the first time, I watched Ron Howard's excellent Master Class, reread Sidney Lumet's *Making Movies,* and asked advice from everyone. One director friend shared that Steven Soderbergh had told him directing was mostly about making choices: "Do you like the red hat or the blue hat?" But the most helpful advice came in an email from my friend the fantastic director Jon Turteltaub. Jon and I first met when I was brand-new in New York City and I auditioned for one of his earliest movies, *While You Were Sleeping.* I didn't get the part—some girl named Sandra Bullock did. But I finally got to work with him years later when he directed a few episodes of *Zoey's Extraordinary Play-*

list. In my first book of essays, I included some advice on writing from my friend and mentor Don Roos, and I'd like to submit Jon as this book's Special Guest Star and share his guidance about directing. While he's speaking specifically about the role of the director, I think his insights apply to anyone who is interested in being a positive and effective leader. Thank you, Jon. If only you didn't live west of the 405, we might be better friends.

Here is 1% of everything you need to know about directing.

1) You know more than you think. Picture how you want it and strive for that. There's no big mystery to this.
2) Sorry, but you now have to work harder than everyone else on the set. Or at least you have to seem to be working as hard.
3) Wear comfortable shoes.
4) Prepare, prepare, prepare. I can't stress this enough. The reason why it is SO important is that it will remove 90% of your stress. If you are going into a scene without any idea how to shoot it, you will spend the entire day freaking out about it and you'll have a stomachache.
5) Nothing goes the way you imagine it will. If you're prepared, that will not be a problem for you.
6) Knowing the difference between what matters and what doesn't is a huge thing.
7) Actors are at their best when they feel loved and seen. You are their audience now. They need to feel seen so it's your job to see them.

8) A mean, difficult actor is probably a scared actor.

9) Laugh at other people's jokes.

10) Knowing what you want and being able to articulate that is important, largely because no one else has the time or desire to give a shit on their own. They want YOU to know and they want to help you get it.

11) Making a decision is more important than making the right decision three hours too late. BUT . . . just because the costumer wants to know what color the pants are doesn't mean you have to tell them. If you don't know, you don't know. (This is also a good time to remember the difference between what does and doesn't matter.)

12) Let other people be right about things.

13) The producer/writer/showrunner wants to direct but is too scared, busy, and/or lazy. So lean on them for how they see the scene while taking the work off their plate.

14) Give yourself an escape in every scene. In other words, always have something to cut to so that you can edit out the horrible and the boring.

15) Actors know when you're lying about it being "good" . . . but they'd rather you pretend it's good than tell them it's bad.

16) In fact, that is true of everyone. Everyone wants to hear how great they are and how delighted you are in their wonderfulness . . . from wardrobe and props to writers and executives. They will love you if they think you love them. Later, when the show stinks, then they will hate you.

17) You can always blow a shot up in editing and make it tighter. You can't make it looser.

18) Tell your script supervisor what you want the editor to know. "This is what I saw as the first shot." "This shot should be blown up into a close-up if possible." "That's the best line reading." The editor will thank you.

19) Move the camera.

20) Encourage your DP and camera operator to "find things" or "search" or "discover something." When you watch the monitor, you can tell them to stop if you have to.

21) Your shoulders are going to be sore. That's from the nerves. Your legs are going to be worse. That's from standing up, running around, and not sitting enough.

22) Make a plan for how you are going to finish your day, your morning, your scene, your shot. You have to keep all this in your head so you don't get way behind.

23) You will hate your AD for making you hurry when you know it's not good yet.

24) This is important . . . Everyone is an individual who wants to please you and do a great job. Help them do that.

25) Don't expect any compliments.

26) Don't invent directing. Just direct.

27) Make your episode the best episode. Don't invent the episode.

28) It's stressful to be late. Don't be late.

29) Pace is a big deal. You have a brilliant ear and instinct for it. Pay attention to it.

30) "Faster" "Slower" "Louder" are acceptable directions. So are things like "Do one like you hate her and see what comes up." But remember, you're not there to be an acting teacher. You're there to direct.

31) It's okay to give line readings (sometimes).

32) When you're reading the scene in the script, you are picturing it on-screen. Whatever you pictured is telling you what to go shoot. If you can, go make that much more interesting than you thought the first time.

33) Other people are really smart and can help. Use them. But it's not an open assignment. Get help by asking . . . don't just let the world offer every idea.

34) You don't need it perfect. You need it good.

35) Move the camera.

36) Ask the writer/showrunner/producer lots of questions about what is important in the episode. What is the scene about? What is the exposition that is important? Make sure you get what they need. It's got to make sense. And if it doesn't, let them know you're confused or concerned that it doesn't make sense. If you don't know what's going on you can't make it work on-screen.

37) It really, truly is good to get that first shot of the day before everything gets way behind.

38) Move the camera.

39) Make a shot list. Every shot you NEED to make the scenes tell your story and derive the emotion you need. Then shoot those shots. If you have a list, you can plan your life and you won't forget things.

40) Be honest with people. People want you to love them. If they feel you are in the mess with them . . . and you aren't competing but you're in the fight with them . . . you can tell them the truth—good and bad—and you will get great results.

I reread the above many times during the episode I directed of *Mighty Ducks: Game Changers,* and every bit of it helped. From my first experience directing, I would only add a few things to the above.

1) In preparation to join the directors' union the Directors Guild of America, I was asked to take their orientation seminar, taught by a revolving group of directors who generously donate their time to lead these workshops. One description they gave of being an episodic TV director was that it was as if you'd been invited to someone's house for a dinner party but also asked to prepare the meal yourself using only the ingredients the hosts already had. You're more guest than host in this scenario, and that was something I may have taken too literally during my episode. I worked hard at fulfilling the assignment as written, and I felt confident working with my fellow actors, and I dearly loved my crew. But later I wondered if I could have been bolder and less polite—if I could have had respect for the ingredients available to me while also feeling free to imagine a more inventive way to use them.

2) Every cast member of *Mighty Ducks* is enthusiastic and professional, and our kids are especially impressive. But as my episode approached, I told the kids that I was nervous to take on this new challenge and it would help me out if they were a little more certain of their lines than usual—a small but significant way to ensure the day goes more smoothly and quickly. And on my episode, each of them went above and beyond in terms of preparation, and they made every day better, and I felt so proud. I think that while members of any team may want to contribute, giving them a specific, measurable request is helpful for everyone, rather than a generic "please do a good job."

3) It is not ideal to direct something you're also acting in. I realize this is a very niche observation, but I think it applies to us all in the broader sense that while you may be a good judge of your own work, it's difficult to see the end result clearly when you are the *sole* judge who is also participating in the thing you're judging.

4) John repeats the advice to "move the camera" because it's such a vital tool in a visual medium to keep the attention of the audience, but I think it translates to any workplace as: make the environment interesting, make it pretty. It helps when surroundings are upbeat and engaging rather than drab and uninspiring.

5) It's a universal truth that people at work really, really love good snacks.

I Feel Bad About
Nora Ephron's Neck

YEARS AGO, I was in Amsterdam with one of my friends, Jen, which is her real name and I'm not going to change it because for whatever reason I have about 27 friends named Jen and even if you happen to know any of them, whichever one you think I'm talking about, you're wrong. In fact, even if I was trying to hide Jen's identity, which I normally might because of the moderate although relevant-to-the-story drug use that I'm about to describe, I'd still call her Jen because calling her that protects her identity due to the number of Jens in my life.

Just as an aside—and I'm not trying to make any of the Jens feel bad—but pertinent to the existence of the abundance of Jens in my life, there was a time when it seemed every guy I had a crush on who I maybe thought for a second sort of liked me too ditched me because he "just wasn't ready for a commitment," then promptly moved on and married a Jen. This happened to such an insane degree that a person (me) could not have been blamed for becoming paranoid or—maybe even in the name of self-preservation—declaring a "no more friends named Jen" policy, but in my experience, Jens also tend to be exceptionally good people, so I marched bravely on, collecting more Jens for friends than I have pens. (Let's not overthink sentences like these, I'm not going to— I owed this book to my publisher two months ago.)

Somewhat related: I once had an old boyfriend tell me a long story about a painful breakup with a girlfriend that had happened years earlier but was clearly still very fresh in his mind, and when I asked him why he still seemed so hurt over it, he stared wistfully into the distance and said with a sigh, "Well, you never get over a Bridget." And the worst part was that, without ever having personally known or been in love with a Bridget, I somehow knew exactly what he meant.

Anyway, Jen and I were in Amsterdam, and we'd smoked pot that day. Try not to be upset about this. In Amsterdam, that's what people have for breakfast with their Pannenkoeken after enjoying a strenuous 8-mile bike ride and doing three hours of yoga—it's all part of their healthy, blond, descended-from-Vikings lifestyle. Although that does let you know that it probably wasn't any of my writer Jens because you can hardly get any of them to have so much as a wine cooler with dinner. (That isn't strictly true—Jenny Han will have a drink if it matches her dress, and Jen Smith will drink a beer because she's from Chicago.) Amsterdam Jen and I had each had approximately seventeen stroopwafels (because, high) and just for the record, Officer, I've been high very few times in my life before or since. But on that day, without a care, there in the square with my hair in the air (March 1st the book was due, and we are well into April), I tripped and fell for absolutely no reason. After I fell, I lay on the ground for a moment in shock. I wasn't hurt or anything, I was just surprised. My shoes were tied, the pavement was smooth, and I hadn't been wildly weaving or jumping around or even walking very quickly. And yes, I was a little high, but not in a way that would have led to forgetting how to walk. There was just really no excuse at all for me not to be upright. I looked up from the ground and said to the Jen that isn't the one you're picturing: "Jen! Gah! What if, someday, I become one of those people who just falls for no reason?" We found this idea so outrageous, so hilarious (because, high), that we laughed and laughed and then probably went somewhere to eat piles of poffertjes and bitterballen until two in the morning.

Because to me, lying there on the ground, barely into my early 30s, falling for no reason was something that happened only to much, much older people. There was a commercial you may remember from the '80s, pre–cell phone, for a tracking/beeper-type supposedly lifesaving device that depicted a fallen senior screeching, "I've fallen, and I can't get up!" This was a commonly repeated and mocked line at the time, partially because the commercial seemed a low-budget production and the line was dramatically delivered by the actress, but perhaps also because no one thought such a thing would ever apply to them anyway since we were all in high school just bouncing around on our pain-free joints with nary a click in our knees.

Then one day soon after I turned fifty, I fell for no reason. I slipped on the stairs I have since had carpeted, and tried to save the iPad I was holding, and the iPad survived but my foot was broken. It wasn't a bad break, but I had to wear a boot for a few months. Later that year while I was on a ski trip I fell again and broke my wrist. I wish I could tell you that—given I was on a ski trip—I was skiing when I fell, which would make me sound daring or athletic, but I was merely walking to meet a friend for lunch. The broken wrist was a more serious injury that required surgery and recovery and physical therapy, and I still have a Frankensteinian amount of metal in there holding it all together.

I'm not sure when exactly it is that you don't feel as young as you used to, but spending a day purchasing specialty items from hospital supply stores might be one indication. I'd never been to a hospital supply store before, but in just one year I went several times to purchase: a giant boot to support my foot while it healed, an assortment of wrist guards to prevent my newly reconstructed wrist from breaking again, and a thing that looked like a massive Swiss cheese made of Styrofoam that provided multiple ways to elevate whichever ailing limb needed elevation. Suddenly the freezer was full of gel packs that could be inserted into various kinds of slings and Velcro-adorned foot wraps, and I was forever driving to Beverly Hills to get parts of myself x-rayed. Even after the injuries healed, I didn't get rid of any of these glamorous items because it occurred to me this could be the beginning of a trend and I might be needing one of them in the future. Oh, and while it didn't require any new accessories, I also had to get an MRI that year after a trip to the emergency room for what turned out to be kidney stones. If you've never had an MRI, it's that machine you may have seen in movies that resembles the drawers they pull dead bodies in the morgue out of, and there is a spooky computer voice that keeps telling you to lie very still in an unsettlingly threatening way. If I ran the MRI universe, I'd ask Tom Hanks or someone cheery to do the voice-over instead of the stern computer man. Maybe I should host an MRI makeover show on HGTV?

If you were hoping this book was going to have fewer kidney stones and more behind-the-scenes stories of what it's like to present at the Golden Globe Awards, this one's for you: the last time I presented, the limo driver who picked me up asked me what the name of the awards show he was taking me to was and I told him and he said: "Is that a show mainly for men?" Perhaps he thought he was driving me to the Golden Gloves or something else boxing-related. Right before I presented (Best Actor in a TV Drama, Brian Cox), I was getting my makeup touched up backstage and the sound on the monitor went out for a second and I made a joke about it and Daniel Craig laughed and I will forever be in love with him as a result. Also, you cannot believe how tall and thin Nicole Kidman is in person. Now, we return to gauging raging aging! (My publisher has assured me not all the sentences have to make sense. They just really need to start printing this sucker.)

As a result of these injuries, not to mention turning 50, I started to think a lot more about what it means to get older. It occurred to me that I had attended Diane Keaton's 60th birthday party (the invitations were printed on beautiful thick eggshell-colored cards that simply said "Diane is 60" in a black old-fashioned typewriter font. I framed mine), an age that seemed impossibly far away at the time, and that I was now closer to that number than I felt, and there was no amount of spa treatments or fasts or yoga classes that could do anything about that.

I'm not talking about the Terrible Horrible stuff whose likelihood may increase as we get older. I'm not talking about serious diseases or conditions requiring regular visits to the hospital. I'm talking about things that are mainly just annoying but also mystifying in that they show up without warning. I'm talking about the moment you realize you've turned 2 P.M. Sunday matinee years old because going to Times Square at 8 P.M. seems like a ridiculous thing to do and suddenly your entire lunch conversations revolve around the best cream for sore joints (Penetrex). On the one hand, this development is okay because you're having these conversations with your friends because your friends have also started falling for no reason and you have people to discuss these things with over steamed vegetables and mashed potatoes because spicy foods just don't agree with you anymore, and in unison you laugh and laugh and everyone makes funny noises as they stand up and return home to their walk-in bathtubs. On the other hand, this change sneaks up on you, and like any sneak, it gives you a bit of a scare.

Of course, I'd thought about aging before, since I work in an industry obsessed with how people look. But I'd mostly thought about it in terms of how strange it is to have decades of yourself preserved on film, and how confusing it is to your brain. If you're not an actor, you choose when or if you'd like to look at old photos, rather than being shocked when flipping through TV channels and suddenly being confronted by yourself at age 30. But the concept that—whether it mattered to my profession or not—this getting older thing was a train that only moved in one direction had somehow not fully struck me until the year of broken bones. That same year, in therapy, I compared my feelings of being panicked about getting something done to Joan Cusack racing to get the videotape to the newsroom in *Broadcast News,* and the therapist looked at me blankly. That my film references were not those of my slightly younger therapist, and that professionals to whom I entrusted my medical care were now younger than I, was another change I didn't see coming. You spend so much of your early life looking up to people older than you and figuring they know things you'll someday know too, then one day you're looking for advice from a doctor who (hopefully) knows more than you do except for not having seen *Broadcast News,* and life's questions become more complicated: can you really trust someone with your mental health who doesn't have most of every Jim Brooks movie memorized? Maybe you knew more than you thought you did when you thought older people knew more? You think, It must be nice to always believe you know better, to always think you're the smartest person in the room. And then you think, No. It's awful. (Niche *Broadcast News* reference alert!)

During the year of broken bones, I reread all the Nora Ephron essays. I am a rereader of: everything by J. D. Salinger, everything by Nora Ephron and Carrie Fisher, and Jane Austen's novels in steady rotation. I don't know what this says about me, but this time, one essay of Nora's bothered me on her behalf in a way it hadn't before.

"I Feel Bad About My Neck" is a brief and funny essay in the book of the same title. All of Nora Ephron's essays, scripts, some interviews, and some *New Yorker* pieces are also gathered in a collection called *The Most of Nora Ephron,* which is one of my treasured bedside table books that I turn to frequently. In this essay, Nora Ephron notices herself and her friends trying every type of shirt collar and turtleneck sweater in order to hide their aging necks. She notices this and then concludes in her sharp, observant Nora Ephron way that it's a shared fate, part of life, and there's nothing really to be done about it.

Incidentally, everything I've read about aging, whether

fiction or nonfiction, has been written by a woman. Perhaps I haven't looked hard enough. Perhaps I have missed the many essays written by men worried about their necks aging because I'm a woman looking to see what women I admire have to say on the subject, or maybe I'm correct that male writers don't spend as much time thinking about their necks as female writers do. I just googled "men, writing, necks," and the first thing that came up was "Why are men so attracted to women's necks?" Thus concludes my research.

I cannot possibly say anything about aging or anything else better than Nora Ephron said it, and I'm not even going to try. It just bothers me that this incredible woman who was a reporter and a novelist, the screenwriter of *When Harry Met Sally* among other classics, a director and a producer, had anything to worry about regarding her neck. She wasn't going to be filmed and judged and picked apart and criticized over it, because she wasn't an actress and Twitter hadn't been invented yet. But still, she worried enough to turn it into comedy, which is what brilliant comedic writers do I guess, especially if they're women.

When my mother's cancer came back for a second time, years after she'd been in remission, this is how she told me: "Well, at least I won't have to get a face-lift." This was her gallows humor, but also a thought I knew she'd genuinely had. Death versus maintaining youthful beauty should not be a competition. Sometimes, a person will tell me that I "look exactly the same." And I always think, No, I don't, and if I did it would not be due to natural practices, and what kind of pressure is that?

In Nora Ephron's essay, she acknowledges that she could have work done on her neck, but that would go along with having to get a face-lift—something she is clear she would never do. So, she resigns herself to living with something that bugs her and moves on. Today, the line is much blurrier. You can still draw a line at face-lifts, but there are all sorts of lasers that (supposedly) tighten your skin, machines that (supposedly) shrink fat cells, injections that (supposedly) restimulate collagen production, "threads," which are a barbed wire–shaped length of some other youthful substance designed to be shot into your face at various points to lift it up. But it will sag again eventually as the substance is absorbed, like a slowly dissolving clothesline. You redo them every six months or so, and if you turn your head too sharply right after the injections, they can rupture.

You might think we in Hollywood all know who is doing what and can therefore decide what works for us, but we don't. The people who know are the makeup artists, and none of the good ones name names. They might tell you what's trending, but they won't say who is doing it. They might call their A-list celebrities "Everyone," as in: "Everyone is loving the threads. Everyone thinks that CoolSculpting doesn't work." Or: "No one is doing that anymore. Everyone is totally over that procedure/doctor/fad."

I wish "Everyone" would just publish their activities to be studied in some sort of medical journal for aging actresses. That way we could all distinguish between what's real and what's fake, what are the results of genetic blessings and what are the results of pricey doctor's visits and then decide for ourselves. Or at least let the secrets to success be publicly acknowledged somehow, like in the special credits at the end of a movie. "The producers would like to thank Restylane, Botox, Thermage, and the Brazilian Butt Lift."

The me that looked my "best" was a me that smoked, was underfed, ran high with anxiety, didn't get enough sleep, and still never felt good enough. And gradually, whatever that machine was and whatever adrenaline was fueling it began to break down, and I just couldn't do it anymore, hence, health camps. It was around that time that I began to wonder, At what point is it okay to stop trying to "look exactly the same"?

It occurs to me that Nora Ephron answers that question in her essay. And maybe there's a reason there aren't as many men writing about aging, and the reason isn't that they aren't thinking about it. Maybe—like my mother did, like Nora did—turning fears about aging and mortality into contemplation and comedy is just one of those things women are better at. And perhaps this is not a burden but should be a point of pride. We get to bond with each other with gallows humor and honesty, a more constructive—even joyous—response to fears about middle life and its injustices than, say, buying a flashy sports car (unless that gives you joy). All the Restylane in the world won't make 80 the new 30, so why not laugh about it? Maybe the through line here is a resigned but cheery: let's all give up! And maybe I don't need to feel bad about Nora Ephron—or her neck—after all.

Marmalade

WHEN LIFE GIVES you lemons, make lemonade, the saying goes. But I didn't have lemons, I had oranges. I have orange trees in the backyard in LA, which might sound glamorous, but when you live in California you know lots of people who have orange trees, and lemon trees, and avocados and bananas even. But this year, something must have happened, some sort of convergence of good weather that was even better than the good weather we usually have in Los Angeles, or something in the air that was less bad than the bad air we usually have in Los Angeles, or the fact that citrus trees are cyclical and yield an exceptional amount of fruit every ten years, which is in fact not a fact but something I just made up in order to explain to myself why I have so many oranges. Anyway, I had a truly obscene number of oranges. In the beginning, they were a fun thing to have. I bought myself an extendable fruit picker, which looks like an overly long broom with a sort of claw basket at the end of it. "Wow, what a badass," my gardener said to me (in my mind). I gave oranges out to people at work. I made orange juice, which I put in mason jars I happened to have for no reason except I got some when everyone started drinking out of them and putting flowers in them. I gave countless mason jars of orange juice to friends, and I even put some oranges in a bucket and left them on the street with a sign encouraging my neighbors to take as many as they liked, but only a few were taken because as I mentioned, lots of people have orange trees in California, and so, still, I had an obscene number of oranges.

The oranges began to torture me. I felt worried about the oranges. All those oranges, just hanging there, not being eaten? I wanted to put them to good use, to give them all a loving home. "You should make marmalade," one of my friends suggested. This seemed like the perfect solution to my orange dilemma. I had never made marmalade before, but a cursory glance at some recipes on the Internet told me that marmalade required an obscene number of oranges, which is exactly the number I had, and I conveniently also now had an excellent use for the randomly purchased mason jars. Suddenly, the world and my impulse buying all made sense, and I jumped ahead in time to the cozy marmalade lifestyle I'd soon be living.

Maybe I'd decorate my marmalade jars with a ribbon and maybe I'd have cute labels made. Maybe my friends would like my marmalade so much that they'd ask for it every year at Christmas. Maybe my jars of marmalade would become my signature gift. "Did you get Lauren's marmalade this year?" all my friends would ask one another. "I've already devoured mine!" Maybe my marmalade would become so popular that somehow it would make its way into a few local Whole Foods and maybe I'd turn into a real company called Lady Marmalade (I realize this is a lazy title for my marmalade company, but this entire fantasy took me about 40 seconds at the time; spoiler alert, it ends soon). Maybe Lady Marmalade would become so successful that I would appear on *Shark Tank,* where Barbara would tell me I was a genius but unfortunately my marmalade competed with her other mason jar–based company, Wicked Good Cupcakes, and so for that reason she was out, and Mark would tell me I was a genius but jam just wasn't his jam and so for that reason he was out, and Lori would tell me I was a genius and she thought me and Lady Marmalade would make a great infomercial and we'd make a deal for gaboodles of dollars and I'd humbly accept her deal but ultimately give all the gaboodles to charity and NBC would make a single-camera comedy based on the school I opened with a bunch of my girlfriends to teach people how to make marmalade for charity, called *Marms!*

And then, one day, I made my first batch of marmalade. Like everything on the Internet, the "right" way to make marmalade is hotly contested, and first I spent about four hours trying to figure out which marmalade guru was for me. I thought having an obscene number of oranges and maybe a bag of sugar was all I would need, but no. Do you have a mandoline with which to thinly slice your oranges before removing all their seeds by hand? Do you have not one but two 12-quart pots to boil your mason jars in? Do you have a jar rack that goes in said pots? Do you happen to have a canning funnel handy? Naturally, you have a steam canner? I don't have any of those things, but apparently Alton Brown does, and you'll need all the above to follow his marmalade recipe. I continued my search, adding the word "easy," and even then, I couldn't find a consensus. Some recipes want you to soak the sliced oranges overnight, some want you to juice the oranges, scoop out the insides, and save the seeds for their natural pectin. Some want you to peel the zest from the orange and chop it and then remove the pith carefully because if you leave any pith you'll have a bitter marmalade. All of them want you to do a test to see if your marmalade is done wherein you put a dollop of hot marmalade on a dish and stick it in the freezer for a bit and then take it out and run your finger through the marmalade to see if it has developed a "skin."

At the end of the day, my kitchen floor was sticky from orange spatter and I ended up not boiling my jar but just throwing it into the toaster oven for a few minutes since the only person I was in danger of giving salmonella to was myself, and I did the freezer thing and I guess a skin had formed and I put my one jar of marmalade in the fridge to "set up," which is where you wait for the natural pectin to gel for a few days, and I looked around my kitchen, which had piles of orange peels on the countertops, and gobs of orange juice pulp clogging the sink, and thought to myself: Why? Why did I do this? If there was no Internet, I might have realized I didn't know anyone who made marmalade and the only way I was going to find out how to do it would be to get in the car and go to a bookstore and the thought of that effort alone would have ended the whole thing right there because I would never make that much effort for something I didn't care much about.

I subscribe to Master Class, where I have taken classes in mastering the art of French cooking, tortilla making, floral arrangements, hostage negotiation, and how to be Christina Aguilera. When does the mastery end? How many things do I need to be good at to feel good about myself? Could Dan Brown really teach me how to write a thriller as well as he does? Do I even want to try? Or has the access to geniuses of various types simply made us feel bad that we aren't enough just being interested in what we're interested in and accomplishing the less-than-genius-level things we already accomplish? Do I need to be good at more things or simply find more enjoyment in what I'm already pretty good at?

My one jar of marmalade is still sitting in the refrigerator. I tried it once, and it had a tough, gummy consistency that was not totally awful but didn't particularly make me want to eat it again. But I can't throw it away for some reason. Maybe

I keep it lurking in the back of the fridge as a reminder: When life gives you lemons, you *can* make lemonade, but you don't have to. You can ignore Internet traps like boiling and peeling and soaking and Wordle. But if after reading this you still want to make marmalade, below is the easiest recipe I found, although it does recommend you use a mandoline (I say just slice the oranges as thinly as you can) and it does recommend you check the temperature with a candy thermometer (or just cook until it doesn't seem too runny) and it doesn't say anything about sterilizing your jars so up to you whether you want to boil them or throw them in the toaster oven or live on the edge and hope you don't get food poisoning! This recipe calls for two lemons and a teaspoon of vanilla for every four oranges, sugar to taste, water (just enough to cover the citrus), and I'm not sure why you're doing this to yourself, but good luck!

- Slice the oranges and lemons thinly, approximately ⅛ inch thick, picking out the seeds as you go. A mandoline makes this process move quickly.
- Place the citrus slices in a medium saucepan over medium heat.
- Stir in the water, sugar, and vanilla.
- Bring the mixture to a boil, then turn the heat to low.
- Continue to simmer, stirring occasionally, until the mixture has darkened in color and thickened to a jammy consistency. The process will take ap-

proximately 35 to 40 minutes and the temperature will read 222°F to 223°F on a candy thermometer.

- Carefully transfer the marmalade to canning jars and seal with the lids.
- Marmalade can be stored in the refrigerator for up to 10 days in an airtight container, or left in a jar in the back of your refrigerator, where it will torture you indefinitely.

Mochi

I HAD NO business getting a puppy. In the fall of 2020, I was on location in Vancouver. I was working long hours on *Zoey's Extraordinary Playlist.* I was staying in a corporate housing–type apartment. The last time I'd had a dog, years ago back in LA—a rescue German shepherd who was six or seven years old and already mostly trained when I adopted her—she would go in and out through the dog door anytime she liked, and even when I had to stop letting her do that because of her tendency to get in tussles with skunks at 2 A.M., all I had to do in the morning was stumble to open the kitchen door in my pajamas for her and flop back to bed. The studio where I worked then was ten minutes from the house.

Sometimes I'd bring her to work, but when I didn't, she had a big yard and a devoted dog walker.

I made all the mistakes people tell you not to make when you're thinking about getting a dog. I was impulsive and unprepared. Canadians are so good to their dogs that finding a place with rescues proved to be a challenge, so one rainy day (it's always raining in Vancouver in February), I drove to Washington State, crossing the border in pursuit of Jurnee, which was the name of the big-eyed, fluffy black puppy with neatly crossed paws I'd fallen for on the Petfinder website. Online dog dating had worked with my German shepherd, so I figured I'd be lucky again. In the car on the way, I heard the faintest voice coming to me from the back of my mind. If the voice were a person there in the car with me, I might have felt the gentlest *tap-tap-tap* on my shoulder. But the voice was so far away and the touch so light, I brushed them both away.

The rescue was run out of someone's house. The woman who ran it had a few other volunteers at the house, and she was taking care of a friend's baby, plus children of her own, so there were people and puppies in her living room, a baby and a toddler in her kitchen, more puppies in a pen in the garage. There were probably nine or ten puppies, but it seemed like more. She'd found the litter abandoned at a nearby Native American reservation and she didn't have any more information about them than that; no idea what breed they were or what had happened to the mother. The puppies had been bottle-fed until they were old enough for solid food and adoption, but eight weeks is early, even for puppies who have a mother.

Looking back, I feel like the rescue people were trying to guide me to take a different dog. Jack was their favorite, they told me, and Jasmine had a cute personality. When I asked about Jurnee, they were vague. "She's sort of . . . roly-poly and . . . aloof," they told me. But she came to me when I called her and I thought it was cute how she flattened herself, legs out to the sides, so she could crawl under the living room ottoman. I almost said let me think about it, but I felt guilty. There were so many puppies. This kind woman had taken them all in, and I was worried about handling just one? Would they all ever find a home? And the rain had gotten worse. I dreaded making the long drive again. With no supplies, no plan, no vision of how this new addition would fit into my twelve-hour days, my frequent travel, I took the offered puppy crate and extra blanket and put Jurnee in the car. She was quiet on the drive home. Thick sheets of rain pouring down made it hard to see. I heard the voice again, a little louder, a slightly stronger *tap-tap-tap*. I gripped the steering wheel, shaking it off. I couldn't give up, I couldn't go back now.

I decided to call her Mochi, which means rice ball in Japanese. I set up her crate in the spare bathroom, and it wasn't until then I realized I'd never had an animal in an apartment before, especially not one this young who needed to be let out multiple times a day. The apartment in Vancouver was on the top floor of the building at the end of a long, dark hallway. Exiting with puppy required: leash, baggies, keys, an outfit at least somewhat pretending not to be pajamas, a long walk to the elevator, waiting for the one of the two elevators that wasn't usually broken, pushing the button, exiting the elevator, going down another hall, hitting the button that triggered the security doors to the outside, heading down the concrete stairs that led to the parking garage and back alley, trying to avoid the area landscaped with rocks that had giant CURB YOUR DOG signs everywhere, which, if you've spent even a little time in Canada, a sign printed in all caps is the loudest you'll ever hear anyone yell, so you take it seriously. Then we'd walk across the concrete driveway where the garbage trucks were always stalled picking up the corporate housing dumpsters, and finally, we'd arrive at a small patch of green, and . . . wait.

This puppy did not like to pee. She liked to sniff and pull though, and every time we saw a dog (everyone in Vancouver owns a dog) it was like she'd never seen a dog before. HI! HI! HI! SHOULD WE BE FRIENDS? I imagined she'd say if she could, to all of them: to the tiny fluffball dogs whom she'd frighten with her giant black puppy paws; to the massive Saint Bernards (not only does everyone in Vancouver have a dog, they mostly have manly, mountain-y, ski lodge–type dogs) who ignored her slobbery kisses; to the people and their grocery bags and the candy wrappers she'd pull from a crack in the sidewalk before I had time to snatch them away. HI! HI! CAN WE WRESTLE? CAN I SNARFLE ON YOU? CAN I EAT WHATEVER IS IN YOUR BAG?! Understandably, a being with this much excitement about the world could not be bothered to do something as mundane as urinate.

My time in Vancouver ended, or so I thought, and I got

her back to LA on the plane with the help of my friend *Zoey* star Jane Levy. Things were a little easier back in LA. I had a fenced-in yard and a dog walker; the California skies spilled far less rain. But Mochi was extremely athletic and independent. She loved to get up at 6 A.M. and chase squirrels up trees and bark at the neighbor's dogs, and she was *strong*. On a walk one day she saw a deer and nearly pulled my arm out of its socket, and she was only six months old at the time. It had been a long time since I'd had a puppy and I'd forgotten how much work they were.

I hadn't expected to go back to Canada, but when I was offered a part in *Mighty Ducks* for Disney+, it seemed like a great opportunity. I didn't love the idea of being away from home again, but the season was only ten episodes, and I'd become used to the manageable two-hour direct flight. I figured I'd just keep doing what I'd been doing: go back to the apartment in the building I liked near the sushi place and the coffee shop I liked, go to the hot yoga place, have dinner with Jane, whose show had been picked up for another season. The commute back and forth wouldn't be as easy with the dog, but I had an assistant at work, and I figured Mochi would get older and calm down and hopefully enjoy barking less and peeing more. We shot the pilot in February and a two-week break was planned before we were to start filming the rest of the season. I went back to LA, planning to return just after my birthday in mid-March. I left clothes and shoes and dog supplies in my apartment and told the doorman at the front desk I'd see him soon.

But by the time *Mighty Ducks* finally went back into production, delayed by the pandemic, it was September 2021. I couldn't imagine risking a commercial flight, so I rented a car and Mochi and I took a two-day trip to the Vancouver border. It was 108 degrees on the day of the last leg of our trip, and no matter how many times I stopped to let her out, she wouldn't pee. She'd hardly had any water either and I was afraid something was wrong. A two-day trip with my dog had sounded romantic and fun, but the terrain was bleak and dusty, the highways stressfully twisty, Mochi uncharacteristically quiet in the backseat. Even though I'd read a half dozen puppy books by then, I somehow missed learning that dogs that age easily become carsick. When we finally got to the apartment, the pandemic requirements dictated that I was to go straight to my place, not making any stops. I handed Mochi's leash to my assistant, Alyssa, and headed up in the elevator. An hour later, she called me: "What am I doing wrong?" she asked me. "This puppy refuses to pee."

During my quarantine I had planned to send Mochi to a fancy dog camp where she'd not only be able to play but also get some training while I was confined to the apartment. After only a few days, I got a call from the camp. "We're afraid something is wrong," they said. They sent me a video of Mochi going up some stairs. Rather than using her back legs individually, she seemed to be sort of hopping on both together, rabbit style. They sent her to a vet, who diagnosed her with severe hip dysplasia. The vet recommended immediate surgery on one hip, a procedure referred to as a salvage surgery. The inevitable second surgery on the other hip would have to wait until she got a little older and her bones were more fully formed. This surgery would enable her to walk but would require months of rehab to ensure the muscles formed properly and didn't cause arthritis later in her life. I was still days away from being out of quarantine, so I couldn't pick her up or take her to any of these appointments, or at all be the dog mom I wanted to be. I felt terrible.

Mochi had her surgery, and we began the recovery process. She was on meds that needed to be administered twice daily and her leg needed to be stretched several times a day and given cold and hot compresses three times a day and my workdays were longer than expected and I wasn't spending enough time with her and every walk I took her on felt dangerous because I had to try to keep her calm so she wouldn't injure herself and a puppy who is not yet a year old is very hard to keep calm. She had a special three-piece harness designed for dogs much older than she was that had two handles I used to lift her in and out of the car and up and down flights of stairs. There was always something I was worried about, something I felt guilty I wasn't doing better. Months passed, and I tried to find every resource available. I found a savior in Anita McDonald, a specialist in dog rehabilitation, and Mochi began spending part of the week at Anita's farm, getting exercised properly and safely and playing outside with Anita's other dogs. Week by week, she started to get better. But I still couldn't shake the feeling that something was wrong. *Tap-tap-tap* . . .

Since I'd adopted Mochi from the house in Washington State, she'd lived in my Vancouver apartment, the house in

LA, a different Vancouver apartment, then a Vancouver duplex I moved into hoping that easier access to the outdoors
would be better for her, and now Anita's house. At times, this
puppy understandably seemed disoriented. One night while
I was watching TV, she got up sleepily from her bed and peed
in a corner that would have been her usual spot on the grass
outside the front door if we'd been back in LA. And one day
after she'd spent the weekend at Anita's farm, Anita dropped
her off and we said goodbye and I closed the front door and
Mochi let out a sound I'd never heard her make, a cry of
heartbreaking sadness. It was a sound that told me she'd been
happier where she was.

I felt overwhelmed and trapped by the choices I'd made
as well as the ones over which I had no control: I couldn't
have predicted her medical issues or the quarantine required
during the pandemic, but still I blamed myself. I was wrong
to have chosen a job so far away, I was wrong to have gotten
a dog in the first place, I felt like I was somehow doing everything wrong although I was trying so hard to do everything
right.

I was driving home from another long day at work on
yet another rainy night, and I called my friend Kathy back in
LA yet another time to tell her I was worried. I was worried
about how long I'd been gone, and worried about things
back home, and mostly—possibly because it was the one of
the three things I felt I could do something about—I was
worried about the puppy. Kathy has been mentioned multiple times in this book, and that's because she has been my

friend since we were 18 years old. Kathy and I were in a college a cappella group, Kathy has seen me through every one of my adult relationships, Kathy is the person I most often ask Have I Told You This Already, because we've been friends for so long and have so many shared experiences that sometimes I can't remember if it was yesterday or last week when we talked or if I've told her the story I want to tell her already or if I haven't yet or if I don't need to because she was actually there. It is a friendship so profoundly fundamental to us both that her son is my godson, and she knows my life story intimately.

"It's okay to give up this dog," she said. "It doesn't mean you're Donna."

I started crying in a way that so surprised me that I had to pull over.

Donna, my mother, died when she was 61 and I was not yet 40. Donna, my mother, mostly did not raise me. She was around until I was about 4 years old and then, after a few absences, each a little longer than the one before, she and my dad split up and for most of my school years she lived in London. I'd go to stay with her for a week or two maybe once or twice a year, and occasionally she would stop in when she was in America, but during these short visits I can't say I ever really got to know her very well. She wanted to be a singer and she wanted to be a painter and she briefly wanted to be an actress. She was in a band called Goddess during some of these trips, and later she was a buyer for a Japanese department store jetting off to France for fashion week during a few of them, and near the end of her life she worked for Burberry in a capacity that wasn't entirely clear to me, but that nonetheless means I feel a happy/sad tiny stab in my heart every time I see their signature plaid. She was striking and glamorous and moody and smart. She was intimidating and artistic and dreamy. She had a laugh like champagne spilling out of the bottle. She spoke fluent Japanese and had a beautiful singing voice and loved to dance and could decorate a room in a way that made it look like she was a millionaire, something she was not. But we never discussed what had happened or why. Even as a grown-up who didn't need the same things from her mother as a child might, I never had the nerve to ask. And even though I'd seen all the after-school specials aimed to convince children of divorce that it wasn't their fault, I still believed that I could have done something that would have prevented my mom from leaving. I never got to have an adult conversation that might have helped me move beyond that.

Puppies are not babies, and animals are not humans, but there were parallels. Even though I loved Mochi, I felt ill-equipped to handle what she needed—maybe my mother had also felt that way. I'd told myself I was rescuing this puppy, ignoring the voice that was telling me maybe I was getting a dog for other reasons, including that things were not altogether well in my relationship and I suspected I might be on my own again soon, in need of some companionship— *tap-tap-tap*—a human problem no animal could fix. And maybe part of my mom getting pregnant at 23 was her hoping a baby would fill an emptiness that was more about her career and identity than it was about having a family; something a baby could not fix either.

I could no more ask this puppy what might be best for her than I could ask my mother what caused her to leave when I was 4, but the permission my longtime friend was giving me allowed for the possibility that sticking with a difficult situation was not always the answer. Mochi had found in me someone who had the ability to handle what she'd needed in her first year. And maybe that was my role in her life—not to be there forever, but to get her to the next place, one more right for her. And maybe my mom knew she wasn't ready, wasn't yet as fully formed as she'd become years later when she had my half-sister, and I'd be better off with my dad. Throughout my life, I'd been so determined to never leave, to avoid following in those footsteps, but maybe in this case—and back home in Los Angeles—that wasn't what was best for me either.

Another thing I never got to ask my mom was if she thought the choices she'd made had been worth it, if she got whatever it was she'd been looking for when she took the path that—especially for the time—was unconventional and brave. I'm not sure she did. But her courage allowed room for mine. Because as painful as the downside was, her determination carved the way for me years later to take flight and go after something that—even for the time—was unconventional and required bravery. And she gave me this story to tell. When I asked Anita if she might be able to fold Mochi into her family, she said yes. She sends me photos of Mochi carrying sticks and digging holes in the snow at her farm. Mochi ended up in a happy home, and so did I.

I once saw a psychic who told me my mother was watching from wherever the other side may be and wanted me to know she could do more for me from there than she could while she was on this earth. As you may have guessed from my earlier stories of astrologers and trying to find meaning in the discovery of small animals in my dining room, it's a mystical message I'm inclined to believe, a comforting thought I carry with me everywhere, a sign more powerful than a squirrel.

New York Is a Person

NEW YORK IS a person. You might argue that cities are cities that therefore can't also be people any more than people can also be cities, and you may be right that other cities aren't people, but I think you're wrong about New York. I have lived in other cities: I have lived in Los Angeles, and Chicago, and Dallas, and they are all cities that are nice cities but cities that are not people. You may dispute this belief, but today I worried I'd hurt New York's feelings, and New York let me know we were okay, same as any close friend I'd had since I was a kid might have done.

Today I had an appointment in the mid-50s on the far West Side. In this pocket of Manhattan—one I'd maybe never been in before—there are windowless industrial buildings with storage space for rent, jam-packed parking lots, and car dealerships. Car dealerships? I thought you had to go to New Jersey to buy a car or get it serviced. It was a chilly gray February day, and I wondered about grabbing a cab or getting on the subway to escape the cold and these bleak streets. I know the prettiest streets in New York, and this avenue was far from any of them. It's so ugly over here, I thought to myself. And suddenly, I felt embarrassed, ashamed to have such a negative thought about a city that has given me so much. As penance, I pledged to walk all the way downtown on an unfamiliar route, purposefully searching out the least charming streets, avoiding the more picturesque path I'd normally take. I owed New York this walk of appreciation, I thought. It might seem strange that I have such a personal relationship to a place. I'm not sure when exactly I started my dialogue with New York, but I seem to have been thanking it, and praising it, occasionally cursing it, and looking for its approval for as long as I can remember.

When I was around 5 years old, my dad and I briefly lived in a fourth-floor walk-up on the Upper West Side in Manhattan right after he and my mom split up. It was a sublet, something temporary while he was trying to see if a law firm that had recruited him would be a good fit. I just remember climbing flights of stairs, so many stairs. In the back of my mind this planted the early seed of the idea that New York was a place that challenged you. We weren't there very long—the job wasn't a fit, it turned out. I remember him taking me to see the stars lit up on the ceiling of the Hayden Planetarium, the real revelation to me at the time being the specially designed seats that reclined so you could look up comfortably. And I have another, later memory of sitting high up in the balcony of a theater that was both cavernous and cozy with an overall warm golden glow. Years later I'd learn the theater was Carnegie Hall. I was often taken out at night by my dad, to dinner or to the movies. I'm not sure if these excursions were the result of his devotion to my cultural enrichment or his inability to find a babysitter last minute, but I loved doing things I seldom saw other kids doing.

We were there to see James Taylor, whose face was already familiar to me from the covers of the albums that were in heavy rotation for a significant portion of my childhood. That night, the crowd went wild over two things: the appearance—halfway through the show—of the singer Carly Simon, and a duet James Taylor performed in harmony with himself by singing along to a tape recorder he brought out and set up on a wooden stool. I didn't know Carly Simon was also a famous singer, I just thought it was weird that someone's girlfriend would just wander out onto a stage, but the futuristic technology of the harmonizing tape recorder blew my 7-year-old mind. I'd already learned New York was a challenging place, but now I knew it also occasionally rewarded you with a magical experience.

Years later, I met New York once again, this time on my own. I was 17 and standing on the sidewalk in front of my NYU dorm on Fifth Avenue and Tenth Street, looking up at the high-rise building I'd not yet been inside and imagining the room I'd be sharing with two other girls. My heart was beating hard and all I could think was I'm not sure I can do this. I've never even shared a room. Who do I think I am? But it turned out that I survived my college years, even though I didn't stay downtown at NYU but transferred uptown to Barnard College. During these college years, it seemed New York didn't care about me much. It was fine with New York if I wanted to stay, but it wasn't going to tap me on the shoulder while I was sitting at a soda shop counter and tell me I was going to make it in this town. New York was going to wait and see.

In my 20s New York wondered what I was made of. These years were a blur of temp agencies calling me to answer phones in corporate offices and catering agencies calling me to bus tables for corporate lunches and serve drinks at charity events and serve dinner at weddings. I spent years carrying trays and taking drink orders and working at my retail job during the day and filling out time cards and breaking in new cheap shoes to replace the old cheap shoes I'd worn out by walking with heavy trays from sweaty kitchens to chic ballrooms, walking from commercial auditions to commercial auditions, walking up the stairs of all the walk-up apartments, walking across the city out of frustration when things weren't going my way, walking across the city for inspiration just like I was doing today.

In my 30s, I began to think of New York as a sort of teacher. There was no other explanation for all the coincidences reflecting me back to me. I was mainly living in Los Angeles then, but I'd make frequent trips back and I would almost always run into someone I knew. At first, it seemed impossible when this happened, but over time I'd learn it's statistically impossible for New York *not* to engineer these chance meetings between you and someone you may or may not want to see. After I moved to LA and returned to New York for visits, I began to interpret these encounters as an indicator of where I was in my life. There I'd be, wandering a street in search of a toasted everything bagel with scallion cream cheese, when suddenly I'd run into that guy, let's call him Blourg, because as far as I know that isn't any real old boyfriend's name who might want to sue me. You know, Blourg? The one with the extensive fedora collection who never called me back? There he is, on the corner of Bleecker Street and What Was I Thinking, when I know he lives in Williamsburg, Brooklyn. "What'd you buy?" Blourg might ask me, nodding his plaid fedora-ed head toward my shopping bag full of hair removal creams. "Nothing, Blourg," I might say, tucking the bag under my soon-to-be-hair-free underarm. "Thanks for never calling me back. Fun hat! Gotta run!" Inevitably, I'd spend the rest of the day wondering about my time with Blourg, wondering what New York was trying to tell me. Because New York doesn't judge, it's just asking you to examine the choices you've made. It isn't New York's job to tell you how to feel. It shows you the signs but not what to do with them. Maybe I'd feel embarrassed by running into

Blourg, maybe I'd feel proud of how far I'd come. New York leaves it up to you. "Thank you, New York, for another opportunity to grow as a person!" I began to say on days like these.

During this time, I started to enjoy New York in a different way. For the first time I wasn't rushing from one shift to the next. I could relax a little and look around. The New York I had access to now was a new New York, but I still knew the New York of my previous decades the best. Now I was sometimes flown into Manhattan and put up at swanky hotels. I was a guest on *Letterman* a few times, and on the *Today* show, events that were impossibly far away from my old New York. And while the experiences were on another level, I hadn't quite caught up. People who knew how long I'd lived in New York would ask me for a recommendation for a nice restaurant and I'd tell them I didn't know any, but if they needed a diner where they could sit and have coffee and a grilled cheese sandwich while waiting for their next audition, I was their man.

In my 40s New York let me appear on Broadway, and as imperfect and complicated as the reality of that dream turned out to be, I felt immense gratitude for the privilege, and made lifelong friends. As I pass through the theater district today on this long walk home, it's the little things about it I most remember. The kindness of the guys who worked at the deli down from the theater on 41st Street, who took care to toast your bagel just so, who waved their hands at you if you forgot your wallet or didn't have enough cash: "You'll get us next time," they'd say. "Have a great show." The resilience of the dancers in the company who would twirl into the wings breathless and sometimes injured. "Are you . . . bleeding?" I'd ask with alarming frequency, and they'd just smile and shrug and twirl back out onstage.

Now walking down Eighth Avenue, I pass a grand entrance to what turns out to be the Moynihan Train Hall, the new Amtrak hub that was constructed to replace tired, old, dirty Penn Station (thank you, Penn Station, for all the train trips I took back and forth to DC, especially when I was in college, but you turned gross and it's time for you to stand down). The Moynihan Hall is a beautiful, airy space, with sun streaming through the 92-foot glass ceiling and a giant art deco clock designed to keep you on schedule from any angle, and perhaps because it's so new, it isn't very crowded. If you have time before your train, you can take in the many works of art or get a salad from Chopt. There are signs that say DEAR NEW YORK, THIS IS FOR YOU, and in keeping with the theme of speaking to New York directly this day, I say, *I love you too, New York!* Outside, overcome, I shout, *I love you and I wish I knew how you felt about me today!* to the people in line waiting for a cab out front. Except no, I didn't, because shouting at people in New York who are waiting for a cab is not a good idea. I continued downtown, avoiding Bryant Park (too green), the Empire State Building (too iconic), and Union Square (too many tempting treats at the farmer's market there).

Normally, I'd then walk through—or at least around—

Washington Square Park, where there are often street musicians busking and people playing chess and vendors selling shish kebob and roasted chestnuts. I usually then walk through or at least near the streets of Soho. But this day, I purposely walked on streets I have no association with and streets I don't expect a lot from, beauty-wise. I walked on streets that don't have memories or bagels or fashions. But there were delis of the kind that have increasingly become obsolete, delis where they only have drip coffee dispensed from an industrial urn, and when you order coffee, "regular," they know that means coffee with a generous splash of milk and two sugars (lots of my memories of New York are local deli–based, it turns out). So, I didn't see as many tree-lined streets as I normally do, but I saw more remnants of the scrappy New York that helped raise me. As I walked through the city, I also walked through so many memories of pulling college all-nighters, and busing tables at work, and pounding pavement in search of work and finally getting work, and all the delis and train stations that kept me going along the way.

Finally, I took a right toward home, on a street that's a bit more out of the way than any street I'd normally take to get home, and saw a couple holding a camera, and as they took aim, I turned to see what they were photographing and that's how I saw my sister in the window of a Barry's Bootcamp having just finished a class I didn't know she was taking. She was visible through the picture window putting on her coat in a muddle of other people putting on their coats. I stopped and stood still, shocked, making sure I wasn't seeing things.

But then she caught my eye and waved and came outside to meet me.

What if she'd hung her coat in the back, not near the window? What if she'd left class thirty seconds earlier? What if the couple in front of me hadn't stopped to take a photo? What were they taking a photo of anyway? Were they on a Barry's Bootcamp National World Tour? Or was Ben Affleck standing next to my sister and I just didn't see him? I mean, really, why would this couple take that photo that drew my attention to the moment I could see my sister if New York was *not* a person who was trying to communicate with me, to let me know it had appreciated my thinking of it today? This wasn't even my sister's usual Barry's, it turns out. One of her meetings was canceled at work, giving her a rare free window in her day, but the class at the location she usually attends was full and that's the only reason she was there. So, on this cold but now turned sunny day we got an opportunity to gab and get coffees and walk the rest of the way to our nearby apartments together.

I asked and New York answered. What are the odds? And you tried to tell me New York was just a city. Obviously, as I have proven, New York is a person. But today, New York was not just any person. Today, New York was not a teacher or a challenger or a guide, even. Today, New York was a person, and that person was my friend.

Acknowledgments

This is my fourth book, so I'm certain I have told you this already, but I'm endlessly grateful to my literary agent, Esther Newberg, for encouraging me to write my first. I'm also deeply indebted to my editor, Sara Weiss, for her encouragement, patience, and for making this book so much better every step along the way.

I'm very proud to be a part of the Penguin Random House family, and would like to thank Gina Centrello, Kara Welsh, Jennifer Hershey, Kim Hovey, Emily Isayeff, Allison Schuster, Sydney Collins, and Andy Lefkowitz for their support. I adore the book's cover and am so thankful to Elena Giavaldi and Paolo Pepe for their dedication to getting it just right.

I mention my friend Kathy Ebel about 82 times in this book because she's one of my nearest and dearest who's been there for so many of life's moments big and small, but she is also an incredible writer herself and an invaluable contributor to this book, generously giving me meticulous and copious notes delivered with her signature kindness and compassion.

I'm lucky to have my sometime screenwriting partner Jennifer E. Smith as an early reader and adviser, but I'm luckiest to have her as a friend.

I'm grateful to my assistant, Elise Laplante, who always keeps things running whether I'm in the sky, in the office, or on the ice.

When my sister Shade Grant read the essay about the health camp I begged her to go to with me, she said, "It was actually much worse than that." I couldn't be more thankful to have her as my most trusted companion in all adventures, be they delightful or hideous. At least they make for a story that's hard to forget.

About the Author

LAUREN GRAHAM is an actor, writer, and producer best known for her roles on the critically acclaimed series *Gilmore Girls* and *Parenthood*. She is also the *New York Times* bestselling author of *In Conclusion, Don't Worry About It; Talking as Fast as I Can;* and *Someday, Someday, Maybe*. Graham has performed on Broadway and appeared in such films as *Bad Santa, Because I Said So,* and *Max*. She holds a BA in English from Barnard College and an MFA in acting from Southern Methodist University. She lives in New York and Los Angeles.

About the Type

This book was set in Bembo, a typeface based on an old-style Roman face that was used for Cardinal Pietro Bembo's tract *De Aetna* in 1495. Bembo was cut by Francesco Griffo (1450–1518) in the early sixteenth century for Italian Renaissance printer and publisher Aldus Manutius (1449–1515). The Lanston Monotype Company of Philadelphia brought the well-proportioned letterforms of Bembo to the United States in the 1930s.